THE

ORVILLE™

SEASON 2.5 | DIGRESSIONS

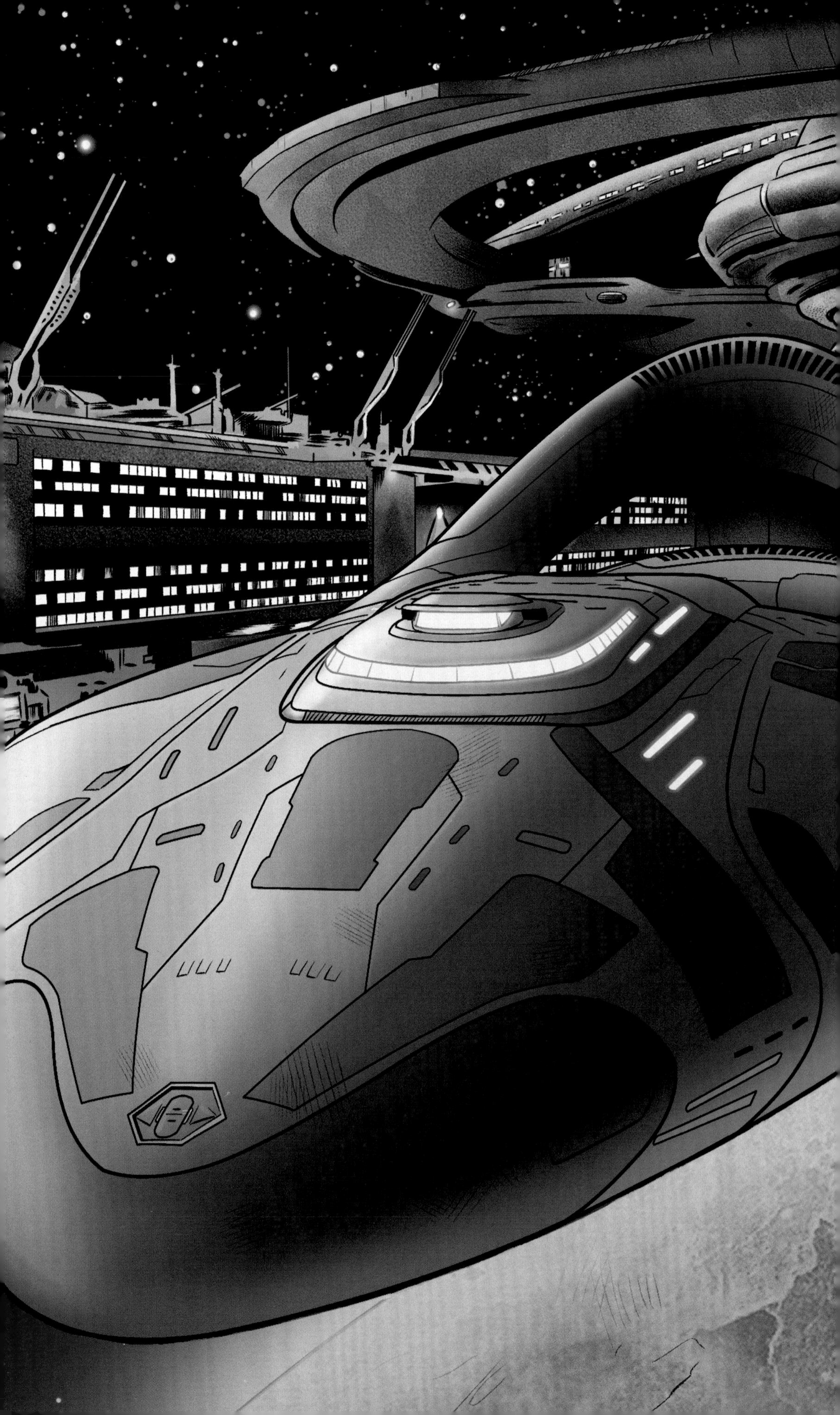

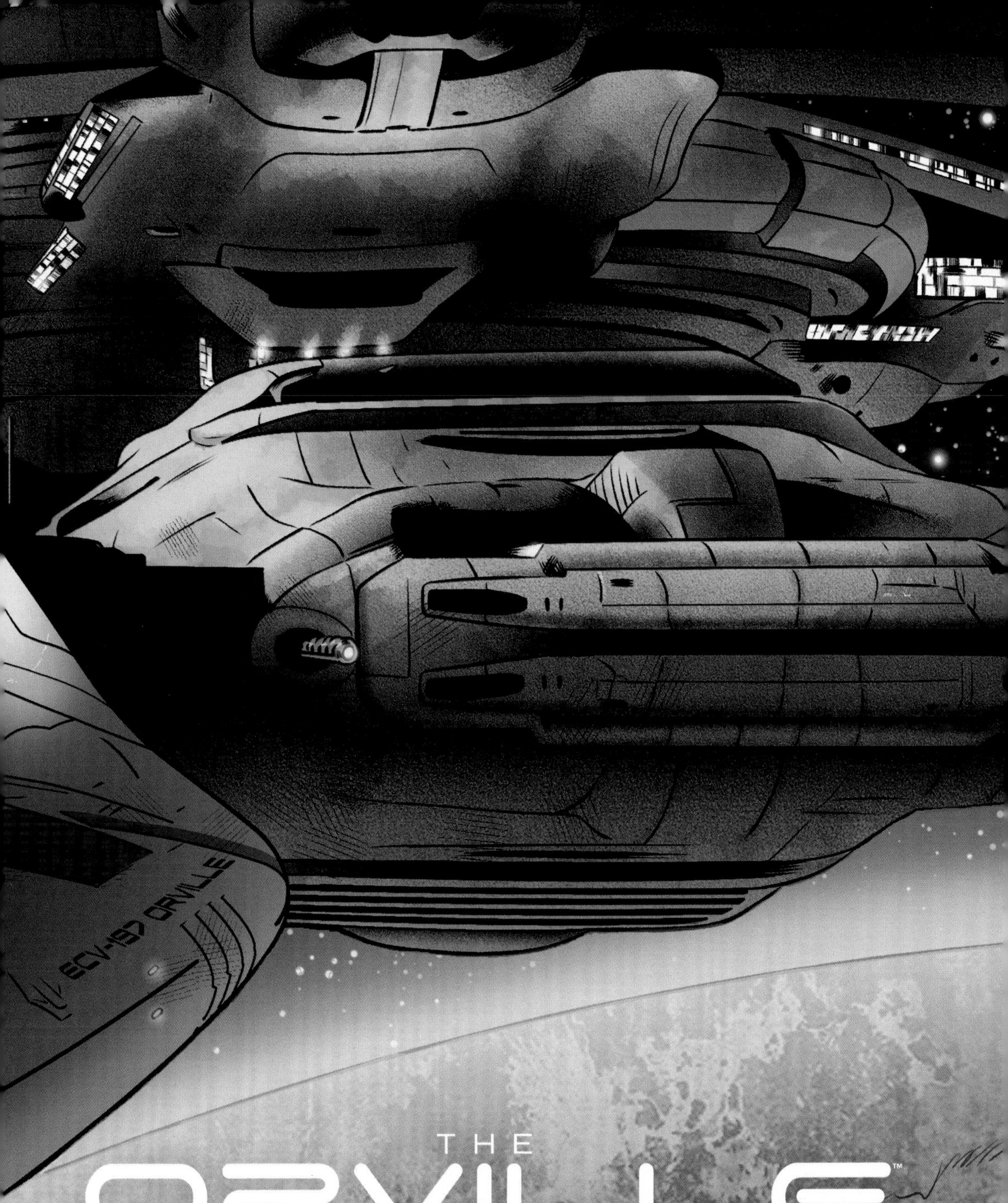
ECV-197 ORVILLE

THE ORVILLE™

SEASON 2.5 | DIGRESSIONS

CREATED BY SETH MACFARLANE

SCRIPT
DAVID A. GOODMAN

ART
DAVID CABEZA

COLORS
MICHAEL ATIYEH

LETTERING
RICHARD STARKINGS & COMICRAFT'S JIMMY BETANCOURT

DARK HORSE BOOKS

PRESIDENT AND PUBLISHER MIKE RICHARDSON
EDITOR DAVE MARSHALL
ASSISTANT EDITORS KONNER KNUDSEN AND ROSE WEITZ
DESIGNER KATHLEEN BARNETT
DIGITAL ART TECHNICIAN ANN GRAY

Special thanks to Seth MacFarlane, Andre Bormanis, Brannon Braga, Gerry Duggan, Jason Clark, Brandon Fayette, Rahne Keith, Joy Fehily, Cassy Brewer, Sheri Conn, and Carol Roeder.

Published by Dark Horse Books
A division of Dark Horse Comics LLC
10956 SE Main Street
Milwaukie, OR 97222

DarkHorse.com

First Edition: March 2022
Ebook ISBN 978-1-50671-140-9
Trade Paperback ISBN 978-1-50671-136-2

1 3 5 7 9 10 8 6 4 2
Printed in China

This volume collects the Dark Horse comic books *The Orville: Digressions* Parts 1 and 2 and *The Orville: Artifacts* Parts 1 and 2.

Neil Hankerson Executive Vice President • Tom Weddle Chief Financial Officer • Dale LaFountain Chief Information Officer • Tim Wiesch Vice President of Licensing • Matt Parkinson Vice President of Marketing • Vanessa Todd-Holmes Vice President of Production and Scheduling • Mark Bernardi Vice President of Book Trade and Digital Sales • Randy Lahrman Vice President of Product Development • Ken Lizzi General Counsel • Dave Marshall Editor in Chief • Davey Estrada Editorial Director • Chris Warner Senior Books Editor • Cary Grazzini Director of Specialty Projects • Lia Ribacchi Art Director • Matt Dryer Director of Digital Art and Prepress • Michael Gombos Senior Director of Licensed Publications • Kari Yadro Director of Custom Programs • Kari Torson Director of International Licensing

Library of Congress Cataloging-in-Publication Data

Names: Goodman, David A., 1962- writer. | Cabeza, David, 1976- artist. |
    Atiyeh, Michael, colourist. | Betancourt, Jimmy, letterer.
Title: The Orville season 2.5 : digressions / writer, David A. Goodman ;
    artist, David Cabeza ; colors, Michael Atiyeh ; letters, Comicraft's
    Jimmy Betancourt.
Other titles: Orville (Television program)
Description: First edition. | Milwaukie, OR : Dark Horse Books, 2022. |
    "This volume collects the Dark Horse comic books The Orville:
    Digressions Parts 1 and 2 and The Orville: Artifacts Parts 1 and 2."
Identifiers: LCCN 2021047749 (print) | LCCN 2021047750 (ebook) | ISBN
    9781506711362 (trade paperback) | ISBN 9781506711409 (ebook)
Subjects: LCGFT: Science fiction comics.
Classification: LCC PN6728.079 G67 2022 (print) | LCC PN6728.079 (ebook)
    | DDC 741.5/973–dc23/eng/20211006
LC record available at https://lccn.loc.gov/2021047749
LC ebook record available at https://lccn.loc.gov/2021047750

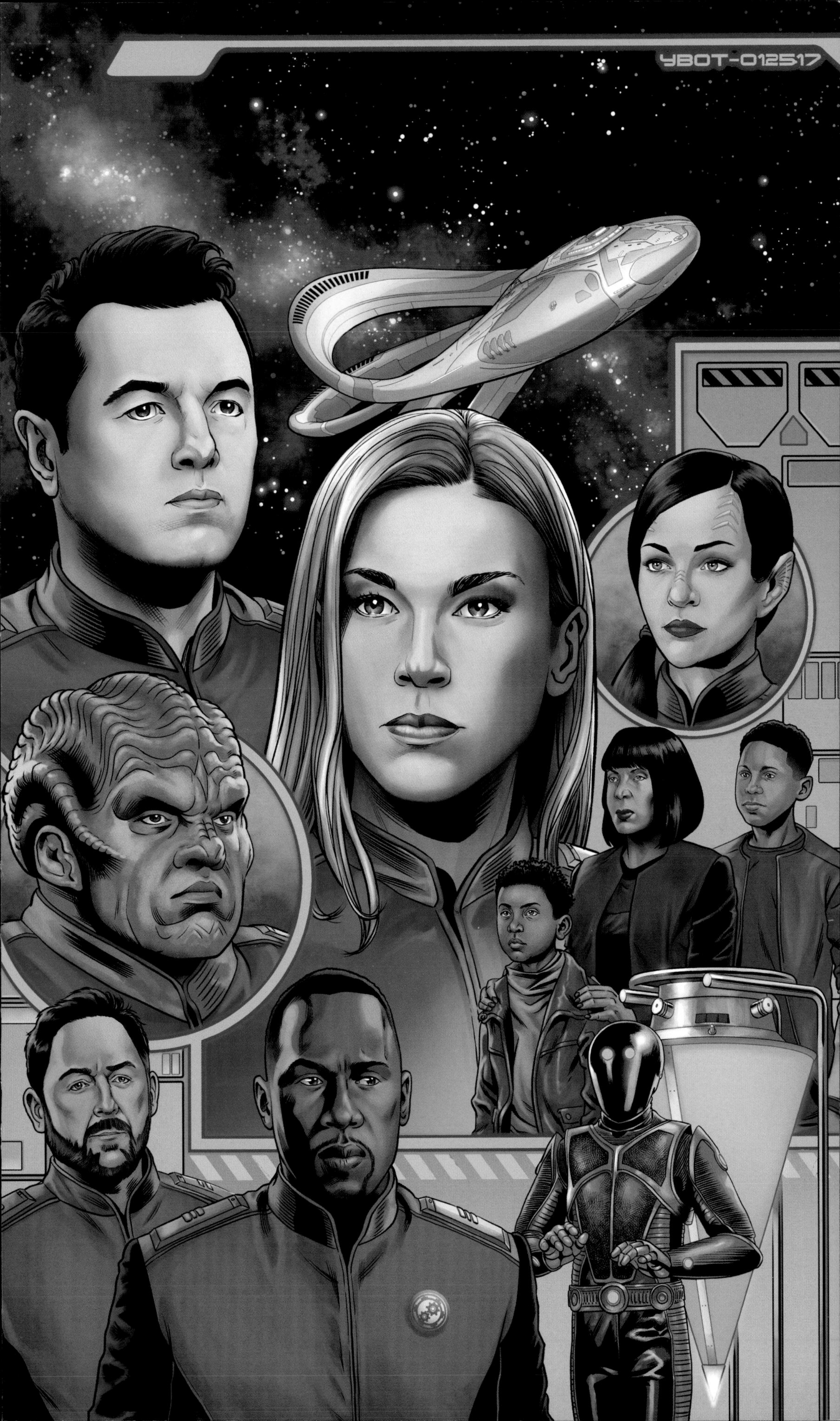
YBOT-012517

DIGRESSIONS PART 1

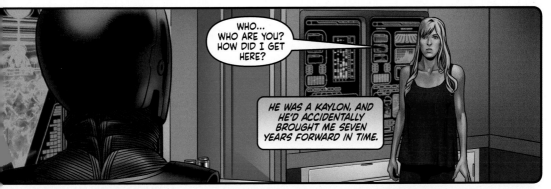

WHO... WHO ARE YOU? HOW DID I GET HERE?

HE WAS A KAYLON, AND HE'D ACCIDENTALLY BROUGHT ME SEVEN YEARS FORWARD IN TIME.

I GOT TO MEET MYSELF, SEVEN YEARS LATER, AND FOUND OUT...

...THAT A GUY I HAD ONE DATE WITH WAS MY CAPTAIN, AND ALSO MY EX-HUSBAND.

MY LIFE HADN'T TURNED OUT EXACTLY AS I THOUGHT. I HAD SOME PRETTY GOOD FRIENDS...

...AND I FOUND MYSELF FALLING IN LOVE WITH THE GUY I HAD ALREADY MARRIED, CHEATED ON, AND DIVORCED.

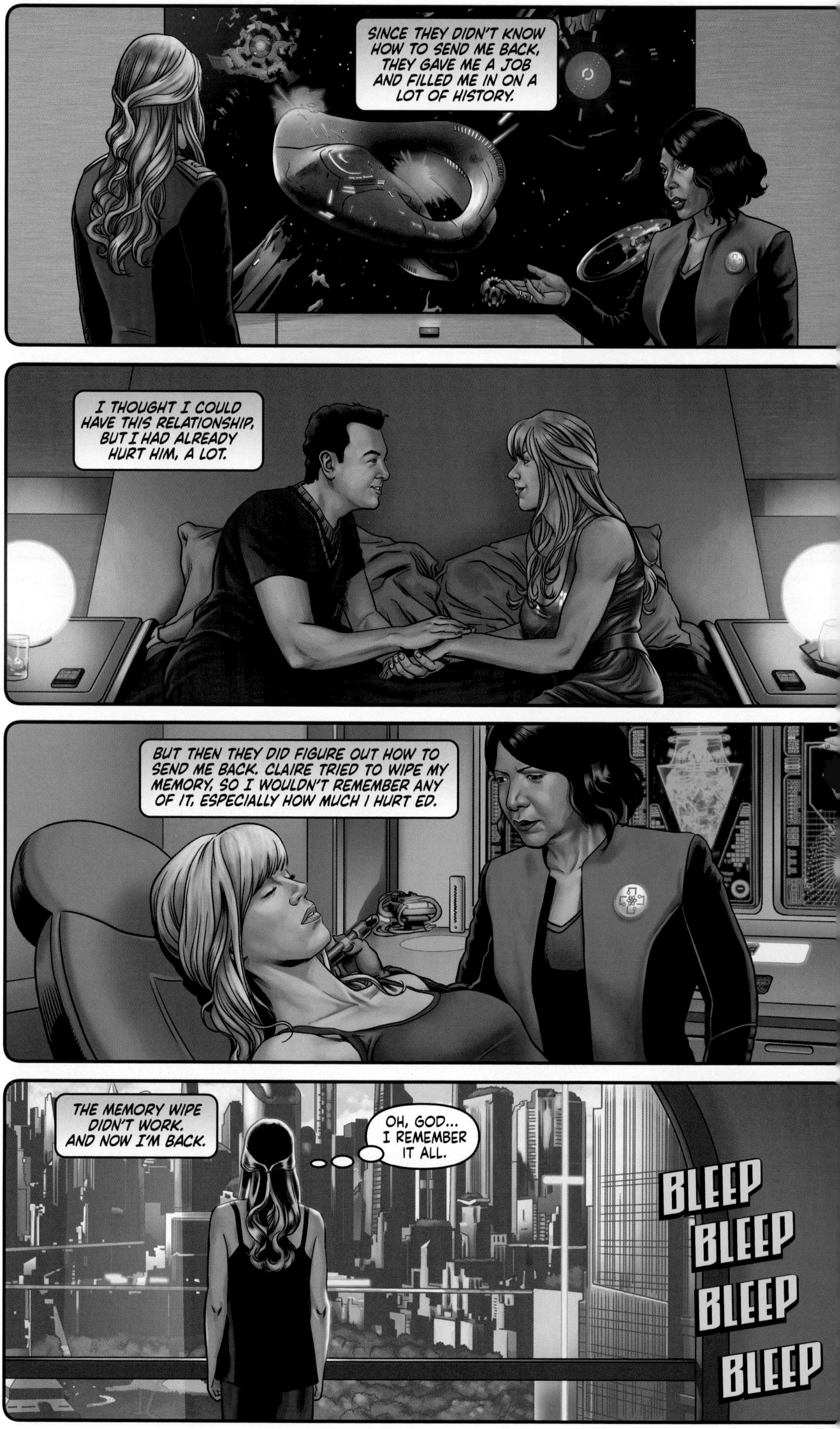
SINCE THEY DIDN'T KNOW HOW TO SEND ME BACK, THEY GAVE ME A JOB AND FILLED ME IN ON A LOT OF HISTORY.
I THOUGHT I COULD HAVE THIS RELATIONSHIP, BUT I HAD ALREADY HURT HIM, A LOT.
BUT THEN THEY DID FIGURE OUT HOW TO SEND ME BACK. CLAIRE TRIED TO WIPE MY MEMORY, SO I WOULDN'T REMEMBER ANY OF IT, ESPECIALLY HOW MUCH I HURT ED.
THE MEMORY WIPE DIDN'T WORK. AND NOW I'M BACK.
OH, GOD... I REMEMBER IT ALL.
BLEEP
BLEEP
BLEEP
BLEEP

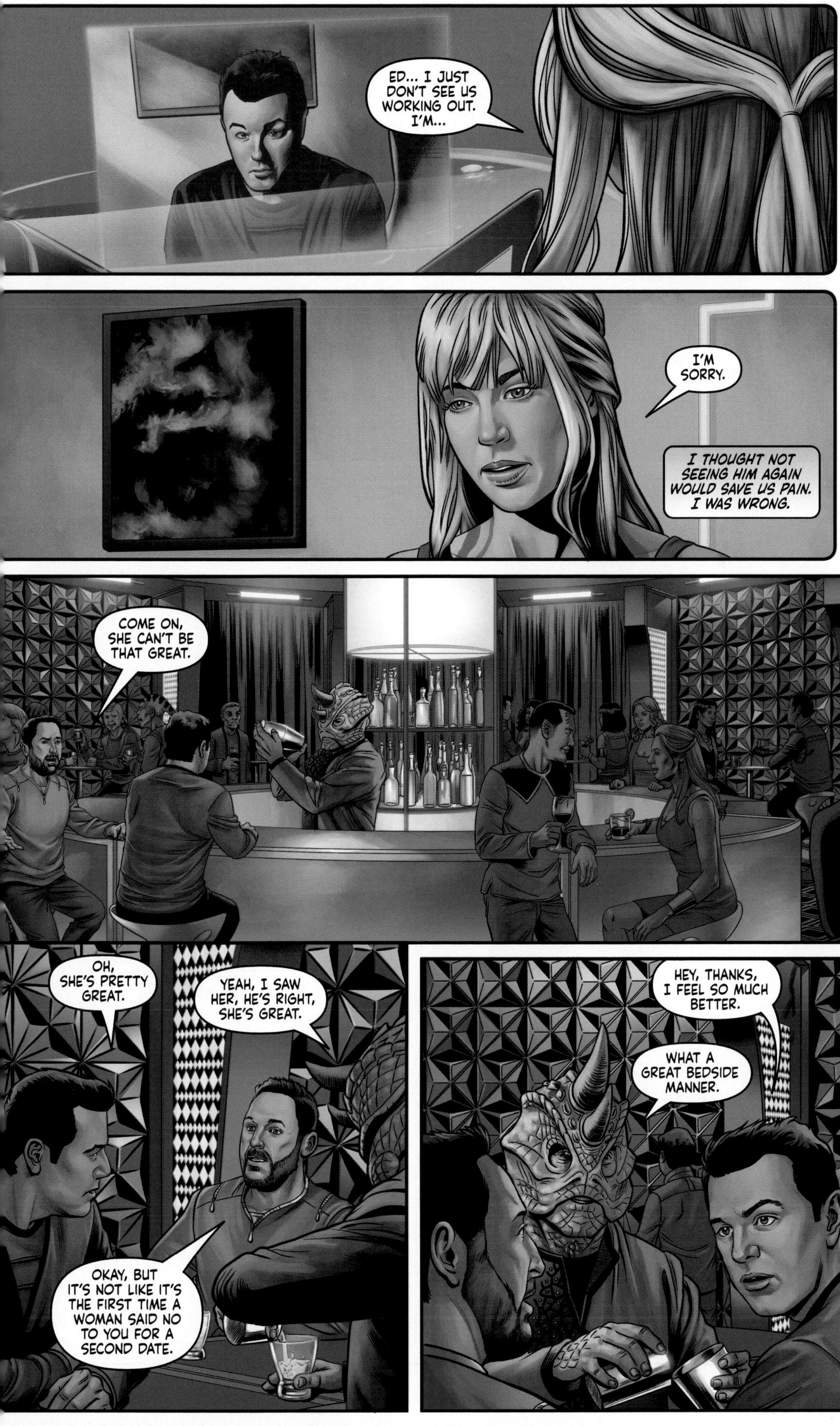

ED... I JUST DON'T SEE US WORKING OUT. I'M...
I'M SORRY.
I THOUGHT NOT SEEING HIM AGAIN WOULD SAVE US PAIN. I WAS WRONG.
COME ON, SHE CAN'T BE THAT GREAT.
OH, SHE'S PRETTY GREAT.
YEAH, I SAW HER, HE'S RIGHT, SHE'S GREAT.
OKAY, BUT IT'S NOT LIKE IT'S THE FIRST TIME A WOMAN SAID NO TO YOU FOR A SECOND DATE.
HEY, THANKS, I FEEL SO MUCH BETTER.
WHAT A GREAT BEDSIDE MANNER.

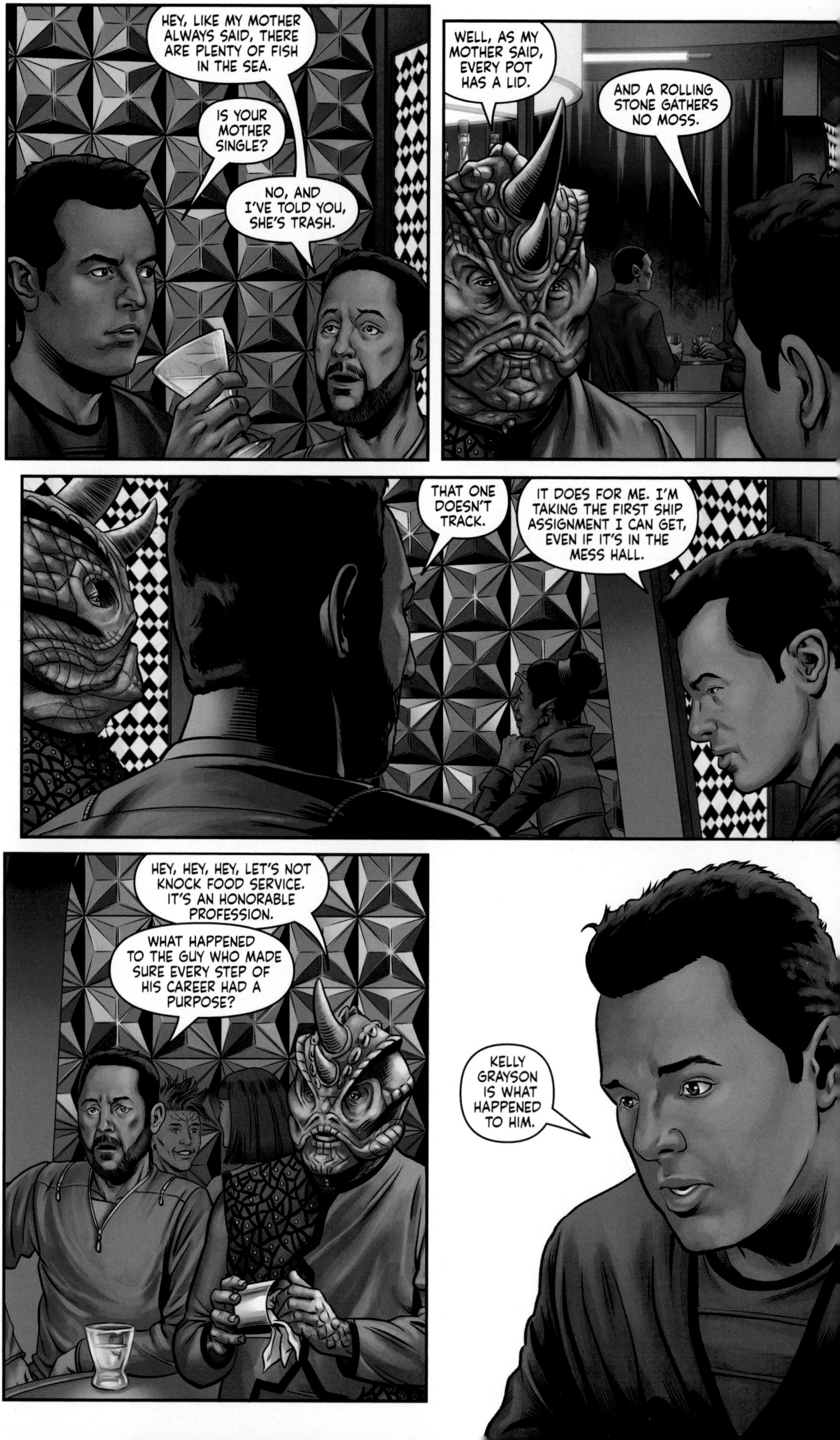
HEY, LIKE MY MOTHER ALWAYS SAID, THERE ARE PLENTY OF FISH IN THE SEA.
IS YOUR MOTHER SINGLE?
NO, AND I'VE TOLD YOU, SHE'S TRASH.
WELL, AS MY MOTHER SAID, EVERY POT HAS A LID.
AND A ROLLING STONE GATHERS NO MOSS.
THAT ONE DOESN'T TRACK.
IT DOES FOR ME. I'M TAKING THE FIRST SHIP ASSIGNMENT I CAN GET, EVEN IF IT'S IN THE MESS HALL.
HEY, HEY, HEY, LET'S NOT KNOCK FOOD SERVICE. IT'S AN HONORABLE PROFESSION.
WHAT HAPPENED TO THE GUY WHO MADE SURE EVERY STEP OF HIS CAREER HAD A PURPOSE?
KELLY GRAYSON IS WHAT HAPPENED TO HIM.

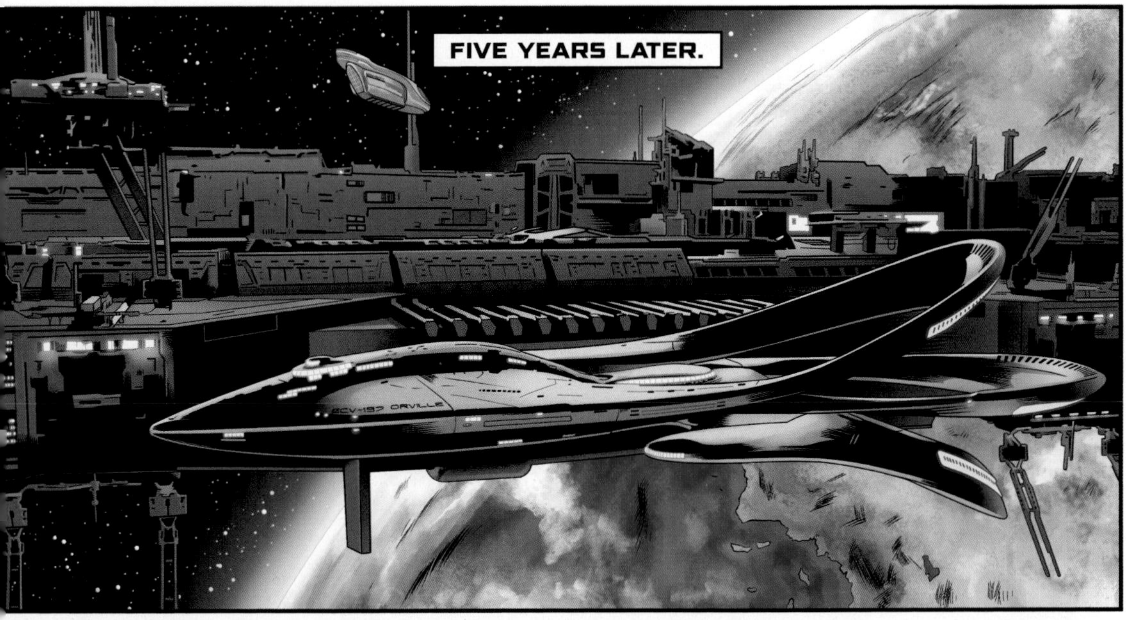
FIVE YEARS LATER.
ECV-197 ORVILLE

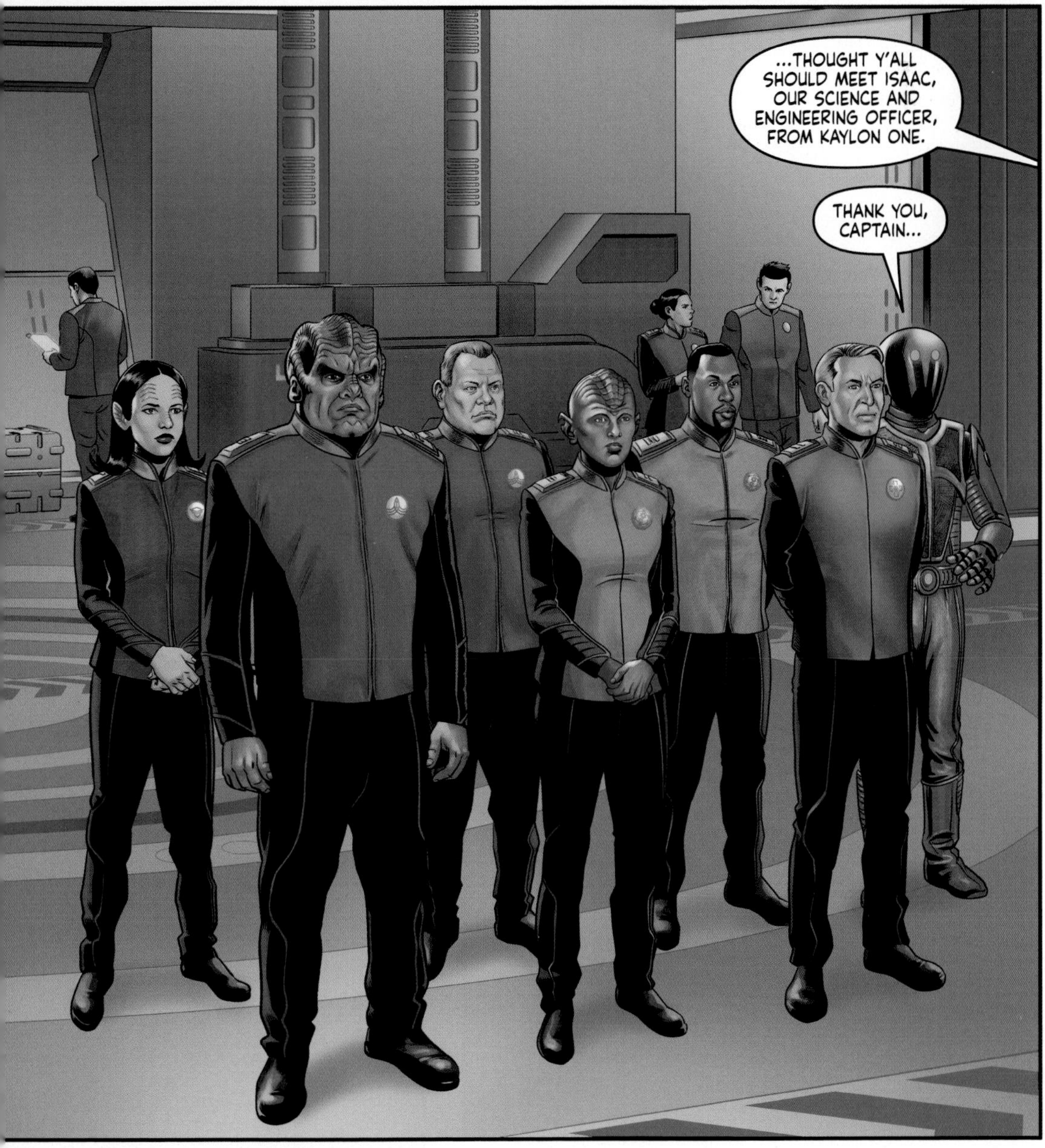
...THOUGHT Y'ALL SHOULD MEET ISAAC, OUR SCIENCE AND ENGINEERING OFFICER, FROM KAYLON ONE.
THANK YOU, CAPTAIN...

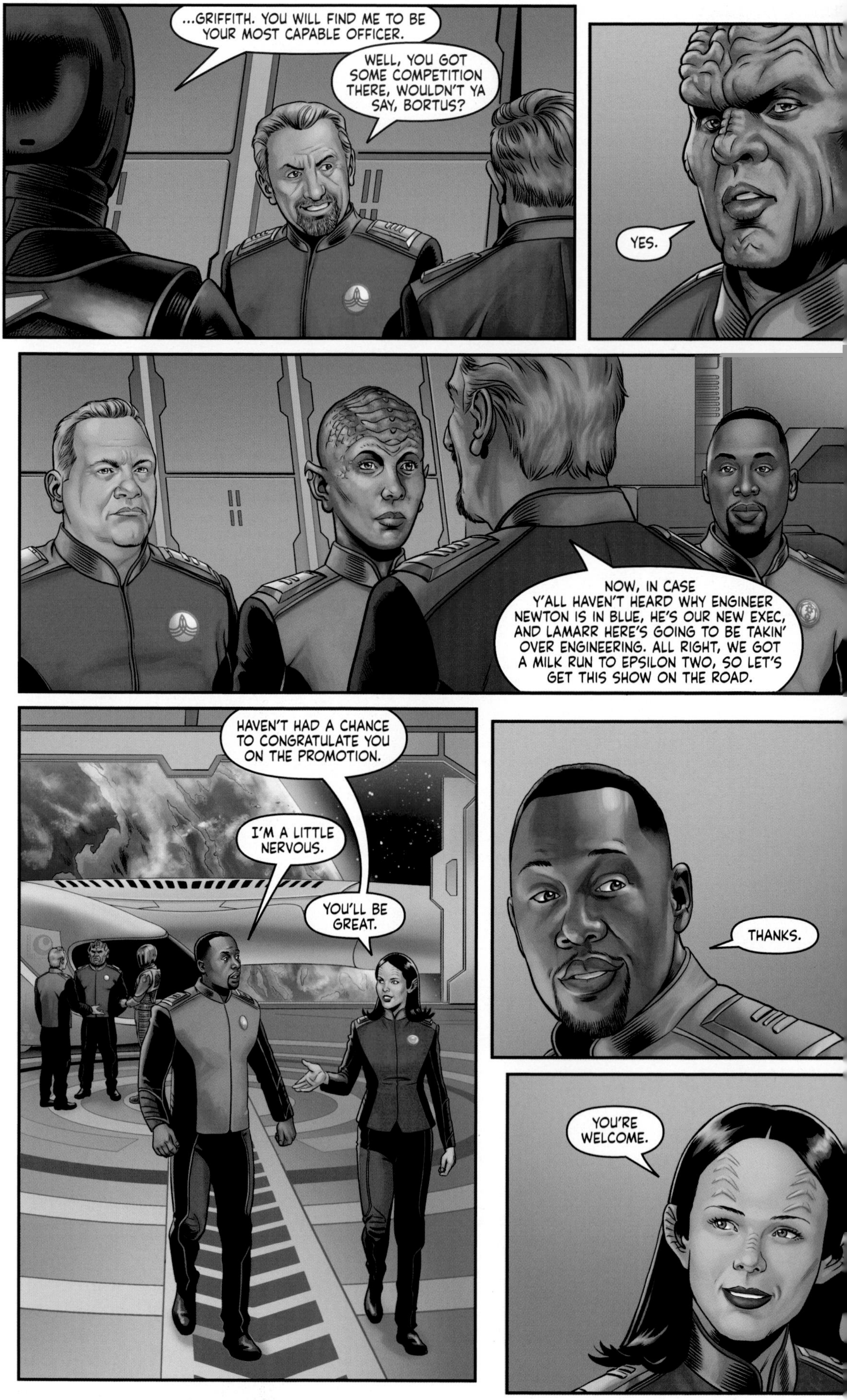
...GRIFFITH. YOU WILL FIND ME TO BE YOUR MOST CAPABLE OFFICER.
WELL, YOU GOT SOME COMPETITION THERE, WOULDN'T YA SAY, BORTUS?
YES.
NOW, IN CASE Y'ALL HAVEN'T HEARD WHY ENGINEER NEWTON IS IN BLUE, HE'S OUR NEW EXEC, AND LAMARR HERE'S GOING TO BE TAKIN' OVER ENGINEERING. ALL RIGHT, WE GOT A MILK RUN TO EPSILON TWO, SO LET'S GET THIS SHOW ON THE ROAD.
HAVEN'T HAD A CHANCE TO CONGRATULATE YOU ON THE PROMOTION.
I'M A LITTLE NERVOUS.
YOU'LL BE GREAT.
THANKS.
YOU'RE WELCOME.

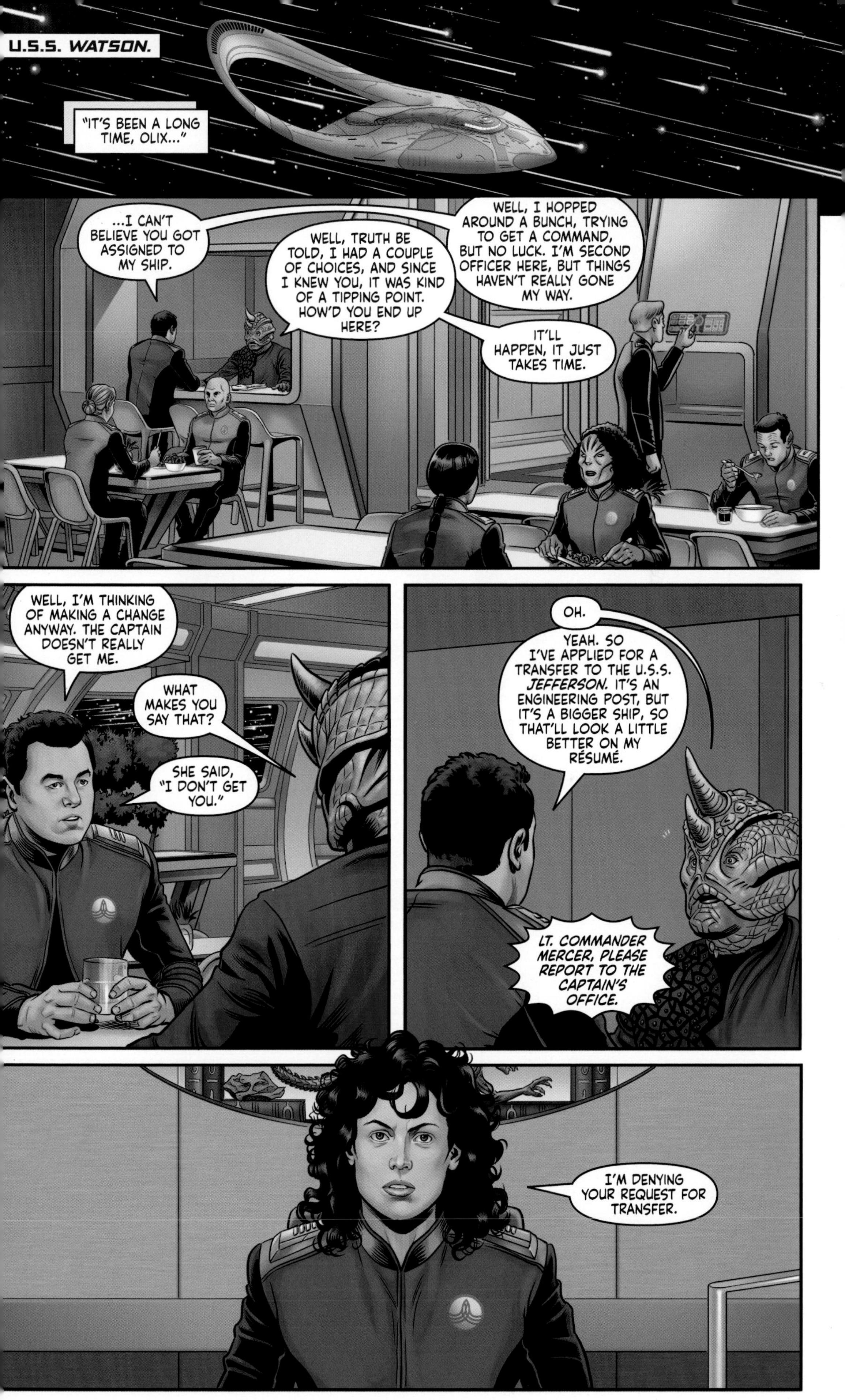
U.S.S. WATSON.
"IT'S BEEN A LONG TIME, OLIX..."
...I CAN'T BELIEVE YOU GOT ASSIGNED TO MY SHIP.
WELL, TRUTH BE TOLD, I HAD A COUPLE OF CHOICES, AND SINCE I KNEW YOU, IT WAS KIND OF A TIPPING POINT. HOW'D YOU END UP HERE?
WELL, I HOPPED AROUND A BUNCH, TRYING TO GET A COMMAND, BUT NO LUCK. I'M SECOND OFFICER HERE, BUT THINGS HAVEN'T REALLY GONE MY WAY.
IT'LL HAPPEN, IT JUST TAKES TIME.
WELL, I'M THINKING OF MAKING A CHANGE ANYWAY. THE CAPTAIN DOESN'T REALLY GET ME.
WHAT MAKES YOU SAY THAT?
SHE SAID, "I DON'T GET YOU."
OH.
YEAH. SO I'VE APPLIED FOR A TRANSFER TO THE U.S.S. JEFFERSON. IT'S AN ENGINEERING POST, BUT IT'S A BIGGER SHIP, SO THAT'LL LOOK A LITTLE BETTER ON MY RÉSUMÉ.
LT. COMMANDER MERCER, PLEASE REPORT TO THE CAPTAIN'S OFFICE.
I'M DENYING YOUR REQUEST FOR TRANSFER.

MAY I ASK WHY?
BECAUSE I NEED YOU HERE.
WITH ALL DUE RESPECT, CAPTAIN, AND SPEAKING BLUNTLY...
...YOU DON'T LIKE ME.
YOU'RE RIGHT, I DON'T. YOU COMPLAIN, YOU THINK WE ALL WANT TO HEAR HOW SCARED YOU ARE, YOU'RE CONSTANTLY MAKING TERRIBLE JOKES...
...AND THE POP CULTURE REFERENCES THAT NO ONE SEEMS TO UNDERSTAND BUT YOU. FIVE-HUNDRED-YEAR-OLD MOVIES AND TELEVISION SHOWS THAT NO ONE WATCHES ANYMORE, THAT NO ONE CARES ABOUT ANY-MORE. WHO THE HELL CARES IF TOM FRANKS MADE A MISTAKE FOCUSING ON DRAMA MOVIES BECAUSE HE WAS SUCH A GIFTED COMEDIAN? WHO THE HELL IS TOM FRANKS ANYWAY?
IT WAS TOM HANKS...
I DON'T CARE. NOBODY CARES. AND NOBODY CARES ABOUT THE LAST TIME YOU HAD A DATE, EITHER.
BUT IF YOU FEEL THIS WAY...
I DON'T HAVE TO LIKE YOU. YOU ARE A SMART, CAPABLE OFFICER WHO GETS THE JOB DONE. THAT'S ALL THAT MATTERS. BESIDES, THERE'S ANOTHER REASON I'M NOT APPROVING YOUR TRANSFER.

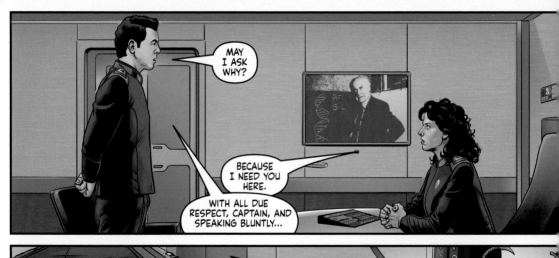

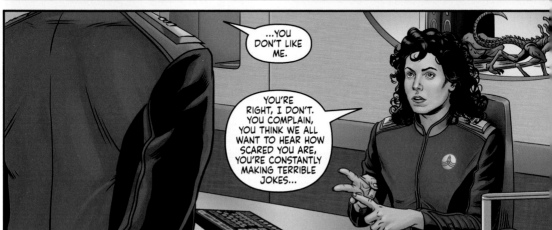

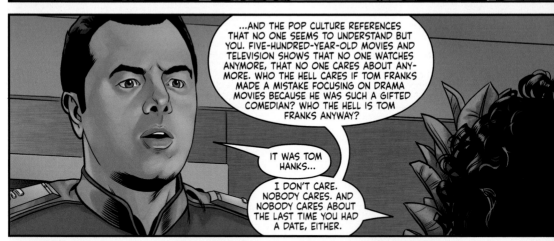

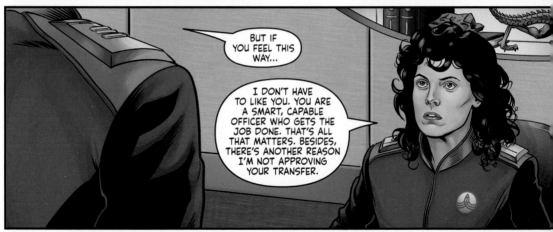

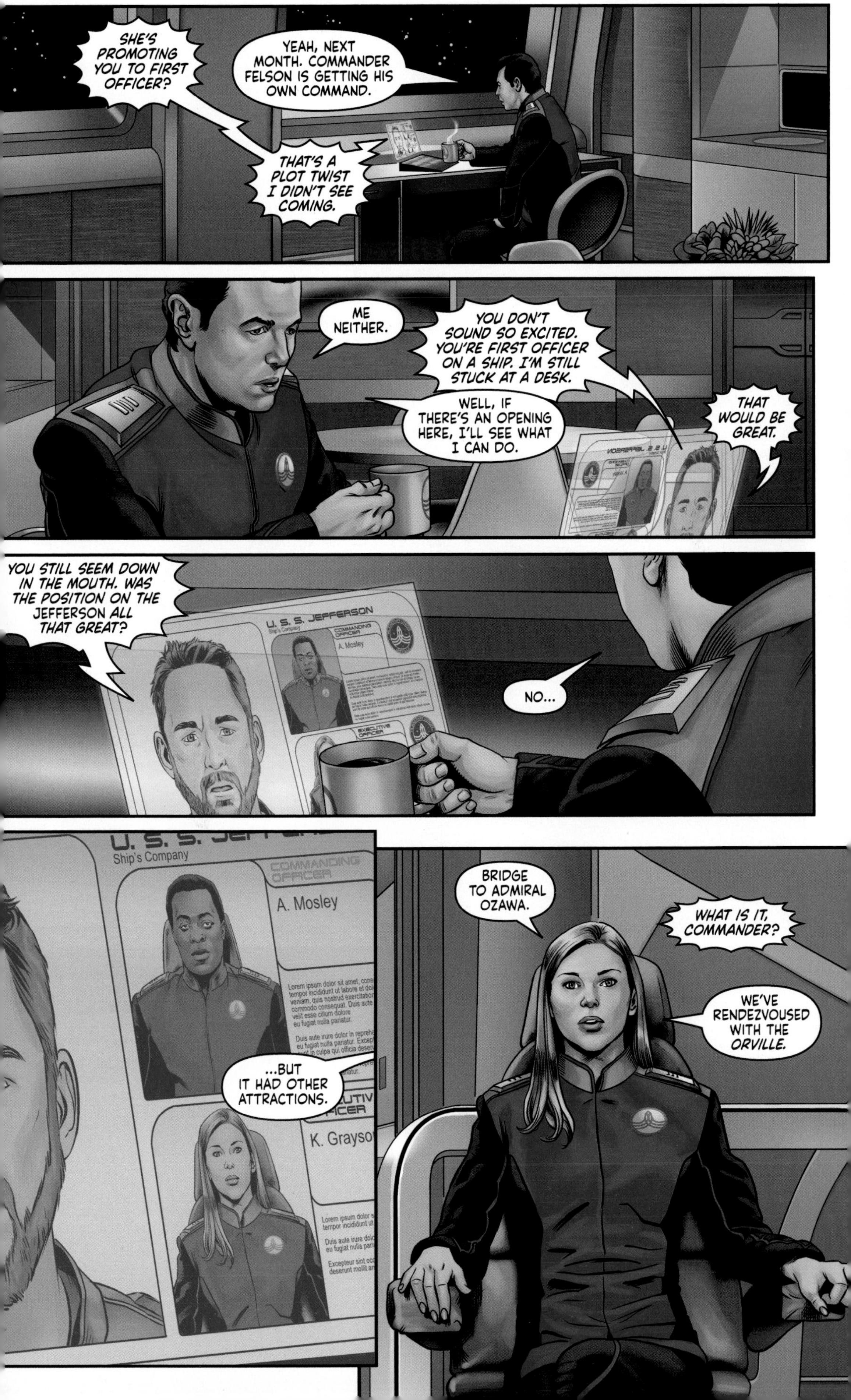
SHE'S PROMOTING YOU TO FIRST OFFICER?
YEAH, NEXT MONTH. COMMANDER FELSON IS GETTING HIS OWN COMMAND.
THAT'S A PLOT TWIST I DIDN'T SEE COMING.
ME NEITHER.
YOU DON'T SOUND SO EXCITED. YOU'RE FIRST OFFICER ON A SHIP. I'M STILL STUCK AT A DESK.
WELL, IF THERE'S AN OPENING HERE, I'LL SEE WHAT I CAN DO.
THAT WOULD BE GREAT.
YOU STILL SEEM DOWN IN THE MOUTH. WAS THE POSITION ON THE JEFFERSON ALL THAT GREAT?
U. S. S. JEFFERSON
Ship's Company
COMMANDING OFFICER
A. Mosley
EXECUTIVE OFFICER
NO...
Ship's Company
COMMANDING OFFICER
A. Mosley
Lorem ipsum dolor sit amet, cons
tempor incididunt ut labore et dol
veniam, quis nostrud exercitatio
commodo consequat. Duis aute
velit esse cillum dolore
eu fugiat nulla pariatur.
Duis aute irure dolor in repreh
eu fugiat nulla pariatur. Except
sunt in culpa qui officia deser
...BUT IT HAD OTHER ATTRACTIONS.
K. Grayso
Lorem ipsum dolor s
tempor incididunt ut
Duis aute irure dolor
eu fugiat nulla paria
Excepteur sint occ
deserunt mollit a
BRIDGE TO ADMIRAL OZAWA.
WHAT IS IT, COMMANDER?
WE'VE RENDEZVOUSED WITH THE ORVILLE.

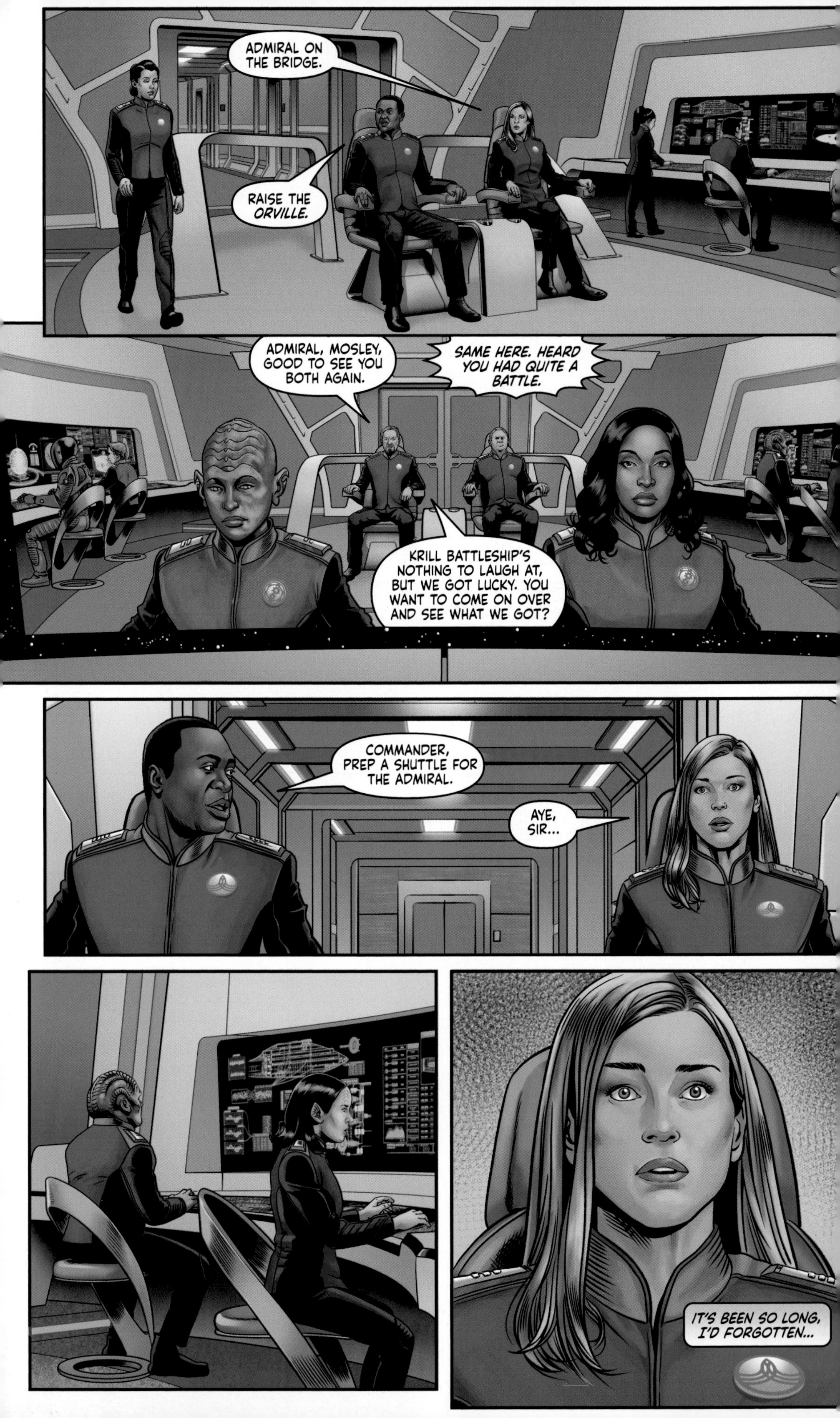
ADMIRAL ON THE BRIDGE.
RAISE THE *ORVILLE.*
ADMIRAL, MOSLEY, GOOD TO SEE YOU BOTH AGAIN.
SAME HERE. HEARD YOU HAD QUITE A BATTLE.
KRILL BATTLESHIP'S NOTHING TO LAUGH AT, BUT WE GOT LUCKY. YOU WANT TO COME ON OVER AND SEE WHAT WE GOT?
COMMANDER, PREP A SHUTTLE FOR THE ADMIRAL.
AYE, SIR...
IT'S BEEN SO LONG, I'D FORGOTTEN...

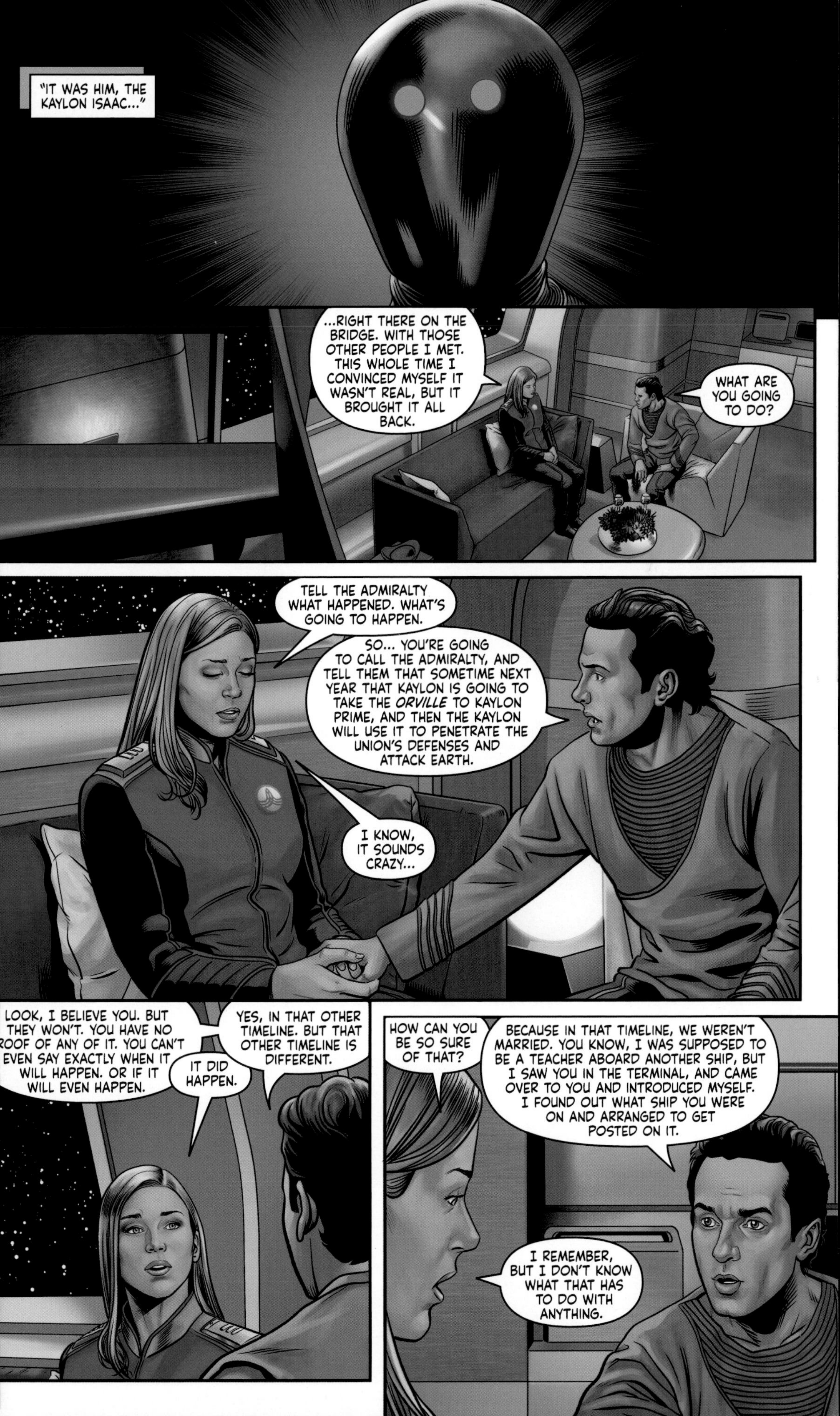
"IT WAS HIM, THE KAYLON ISAAC..."
...RIGHT THERE ON THE BRIDGE. WITH THOSE OTHER PEOPLE I MET. THIS WHOLE TIME I CONVINCED MYSELF IT WASN'T REAL, BUT IT BROUGHT IT ALL BACK.
WHAT ARE YOU GOING TO DO?
TELL THE ADMIRALTY WHAT HAPPENED. WHAT'S GOING TO HAPPEN.
SO... YOU'RE GOING TO CALL THE ADMIRALTY, AND TELL THEM THAT SOMETIME NEXT YEAR THAT KAYLON IS GOING TO TAKE THE *ORVILLE* TO KAYLON PRIME, AND THEN THE KAYLON WILL USE IT TO PENETRATE THE UNION'S DEFENSES AND ATTACK EARTH.
I KNOW, IT SOUNDS CRAZY...
LOOK, I BELIEVE YOU. BUT THEY WON'T. YOU HAVE NO ROOF OF ANY OF IT. YOU CAN'T EVEN SAY EXACTLY WHEN IT WILL HAPPEN. OR IF IT WILL EVEN HAPPEN.
IT DID HAPPEN.
YES, IN THAT OTHER TIMELINE. BUT THAT OTHER TIMELINE IS DIFFERENT.
HOW CAN YOU BE SO SURE OF THAT?
BECAUSE IN THAT TIMELINE, WE WEREN'T MARRIED. YOU KNOW, I WAS SUPPOSED TO BE A TEACHER ABOARD ANOTHER SHIP, BUT I SAW YOU IN THE TERMINAL, AND CAME OVER TO YOU AND INTRODUCED MYSELF. I FOUND OUT WHAT SHIP YOU WERE ON AND ARRANGED TO GET POSTED ON IT.
I REMEMBER, BUT I DON'T KNOW WHAT THAT HAS TO DO WITH ANYTHING.

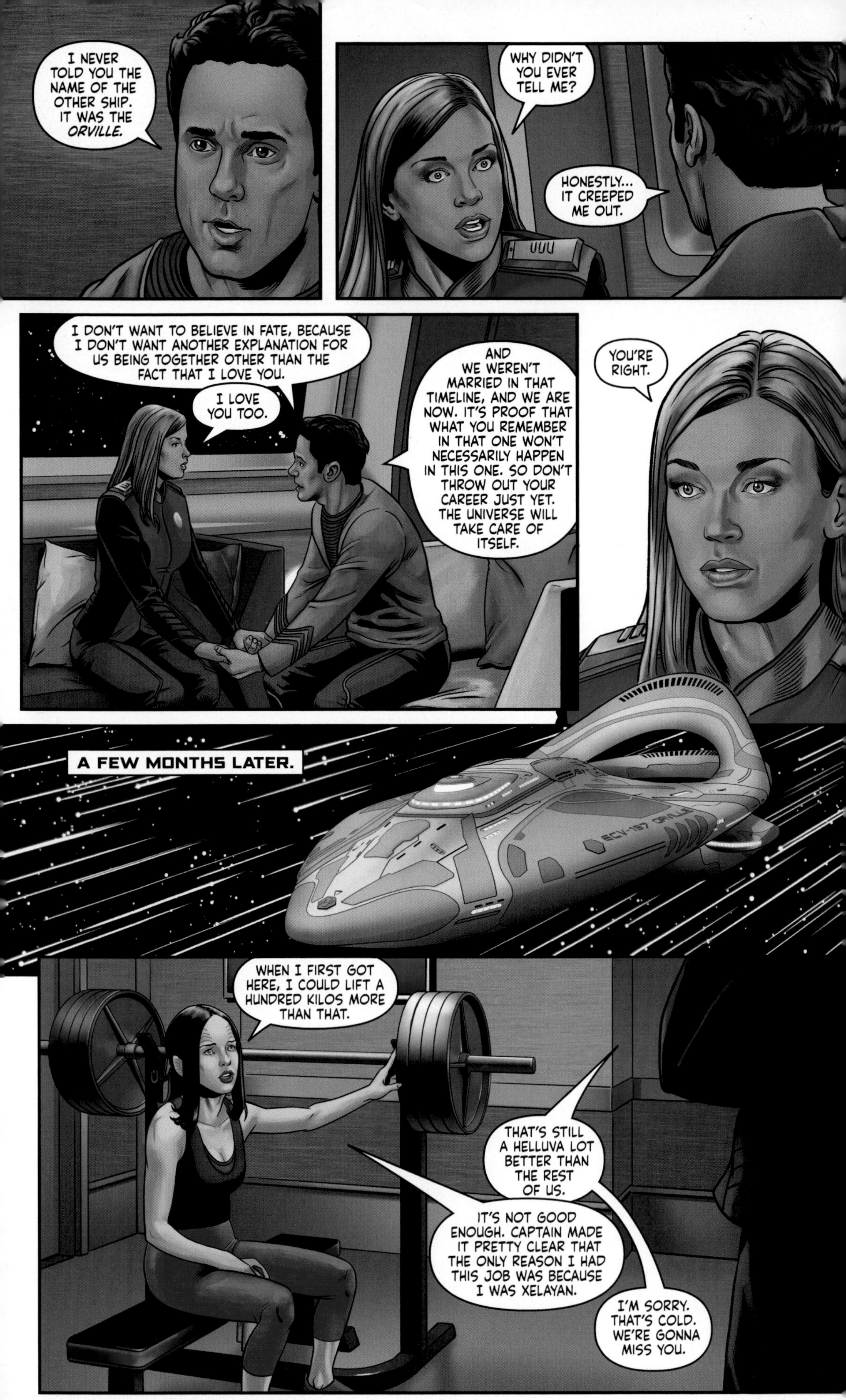
I NEVER TOLD YOU THE NAME OF THE OTHER SHIP. IT WAS THE *ORVILLE.*
WHY DIDN'T YOU EVER TELL ME?
HONESTLY... IT CREEPED ME OUT.
I DON'T WANT TO BELIEVE IN FATE, BECAUSE I DON'T WANT ANOTHER EXPLANATION FOR US BEING TOGETHER OTHER THAN THE FACT THAT I LOVE YOU.
I LOVE YOU TOO.
AND WE WEREN'T MARRIED IN THAT TIMELINE, AND WE ARE NOW. IT'S PROOF THAT WHAT YOU REMEMBER IN THAT ONE WON'T NECESSARILY HAPPEN IN THIS ONE. SO DON'T THROW OUT YOUR CAREER JUST YET. THE UNIVERSE WILL TAKE CARE OF ITSELF.
YOU'RE RIGHT.
A FEW MONTHS LATER.
ECV-197 ORVILLE
WHEN I FIRST GOT HERE, I COULD LIFT A HUNDRED KILOS MORE THAN THAT.
THAT'S STILL A HELLUVA LOT BETTER THAN THE REST OF US.
IT'S NOT GOOD ENOUGH. CAPTAIN MADE IT PRETTY CLEAR THAT THE ONLY REASON I HAD THIS JOB WAS BECAUSE I WAS XELAYAN.
I'M SORRY. THAT'S COLD. WE'RE GONNA MISS YOU.

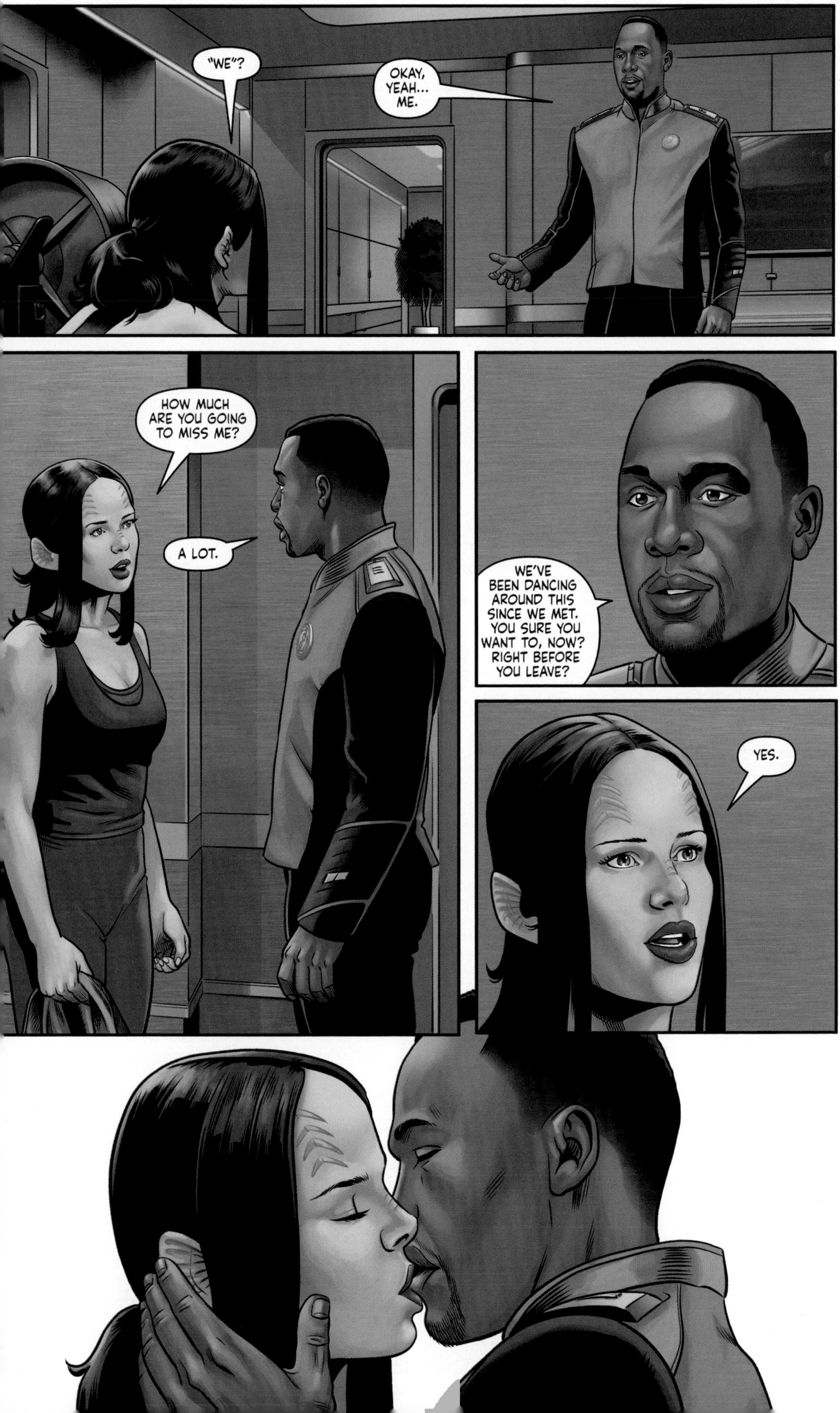
"WE"?
OKAY, YEAH... ME.
HOW MUCH ARE YOU GOING TO MISS ME?
A LOT.
WE'VE BEEN DANCING AROUND THIS SINCE WE MET. YOU SURE YOU WANT TO, NOW? RIGHT BEFORE YOU LEAVE?
YES.

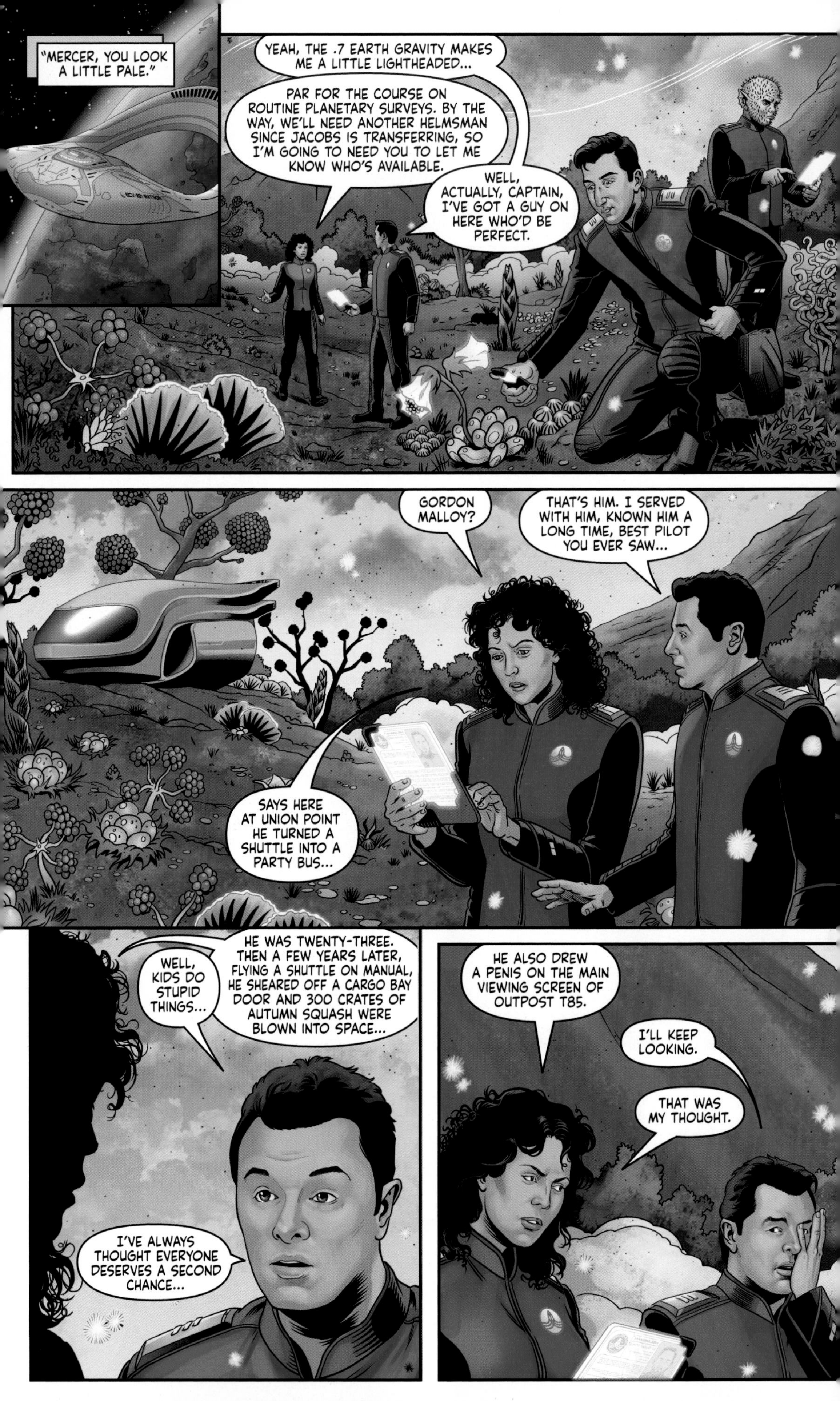
"MERCER, YOU LOOK A LITTLE PALE."
YEAH, THE .7 EARTH GRAVITY MAKES ME A LITTLE LIGHTHEADED...
PAR FOR THE COURSE ON ROUTINE PLANETARY SURVEYS. BY THE WAY, WE'LL NEED ANOTHER HELMSMAN SINCE JACOBS IS TRANSFERRING, SO I'M GOING TO NEED YOU TO LET ME KNOW WHO'S AVAILABLE.
WELL, ACTUALLY, CAPTAIN, I'VE GOT A GUY ON HERE WHO'D BE PERFECT.
GORDON MALLOY?
THAT'S HIM. I SERVED WITH HIM, KNOWN HIM A LONG TIME, BEST PILOT YOU EVER SAW...
SAYS HERE AT UNION POINT HE TURNED A SHUTTLE INTO A PARTY BUS...
WELL, KIDS DO STUPID THINGS...
HE WAS TWENTY-THREE. THEN A FEW YEARS LATER, FLYING A SHUTTLE ON MANUAL, HE SHEARED OFF A CARGO BAY DOOR AND 300 CRATES OF AUTUMN SQUASH WERE BLOWN INTO SPACE...
I'VE ALWAYS THOUGHT EVERYONE DESERVES A SECOND CHANCE...
HE ALSO DREW A PENIS ON THE MAIN VIEWING SCREEN OF OUTPOST T85.
I'LL KEEP LOOKING.
THAT WAS MY THOUGHT.

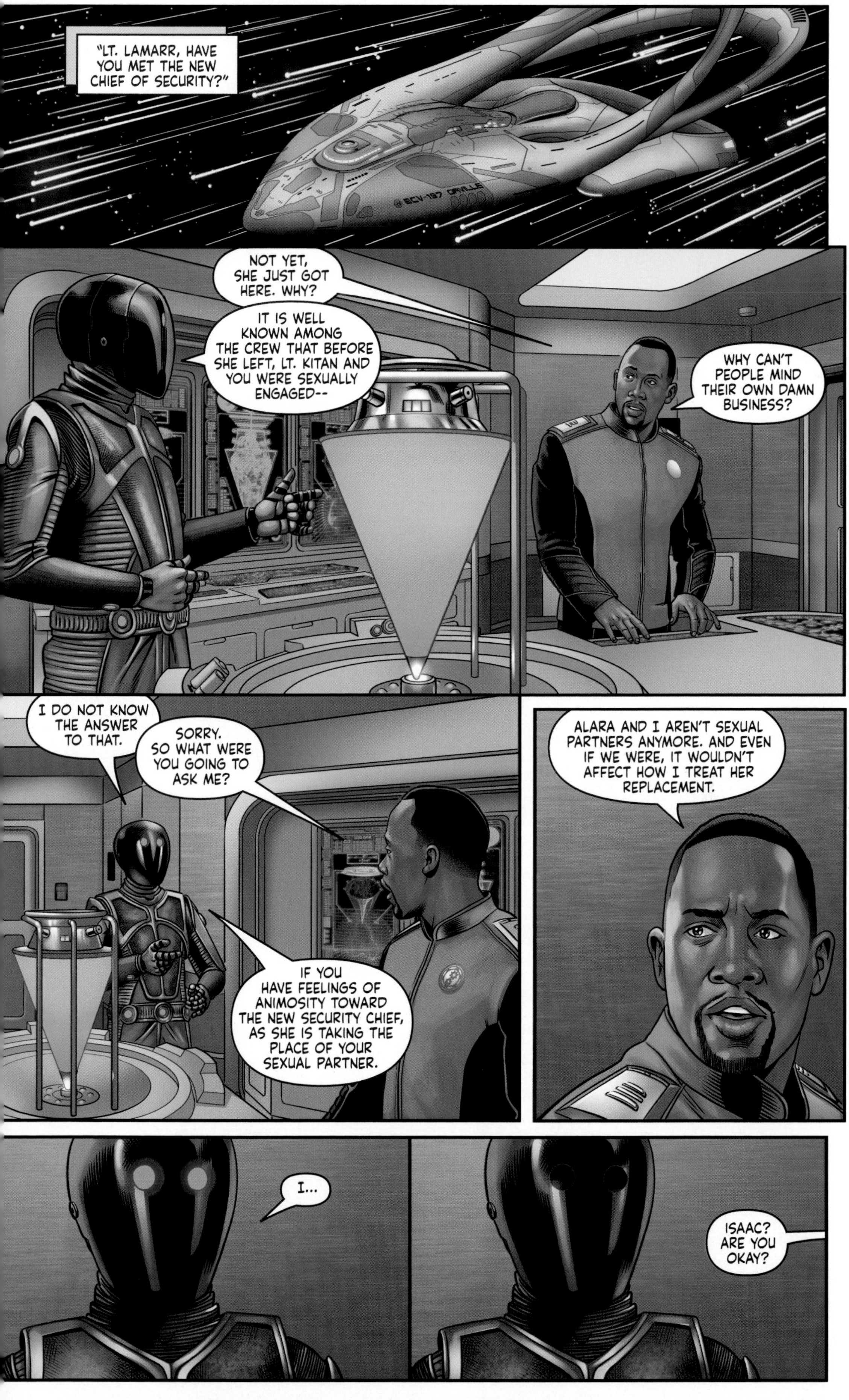
"LT. LAMARR, HAVE YOU MET THE NEW CHIEF OF SECURITY?"
ECV-197 ORVILLE
NOT YET, SHE JUST GOT HERE. WHY?
IT IS WELL KNOWN AMONG THE CREW THAT BEFORE SHE LEFT, LT. KITAN AND YOU WERE SEXUALLY ENGAGED--
WHY CAN'T PEOPLE MIND THEIR OWN DAMN BUSINESS?
I DO NOT KNOW THE ANSWER TO THAT.
SORRY. SO WHAT WERE YOU GOING TO ASK ME?
IF YOU HAVE FEELINGS OF ANIMOSITY TOWARD THE NEW SECURITY CHIEF, AS SHE IS TAKING THE PLACE OF YOUR SEXUAL PARTNER.
ALARA AND I AREN'T SEXUAL PARTNERS ANYMORE. AND EVEN IF WE WERE, IT WOULDN'T AFFECT HOW I TREAT HER REPLACEMENT.
I...
ISAAC? ARE YOU OKAY?

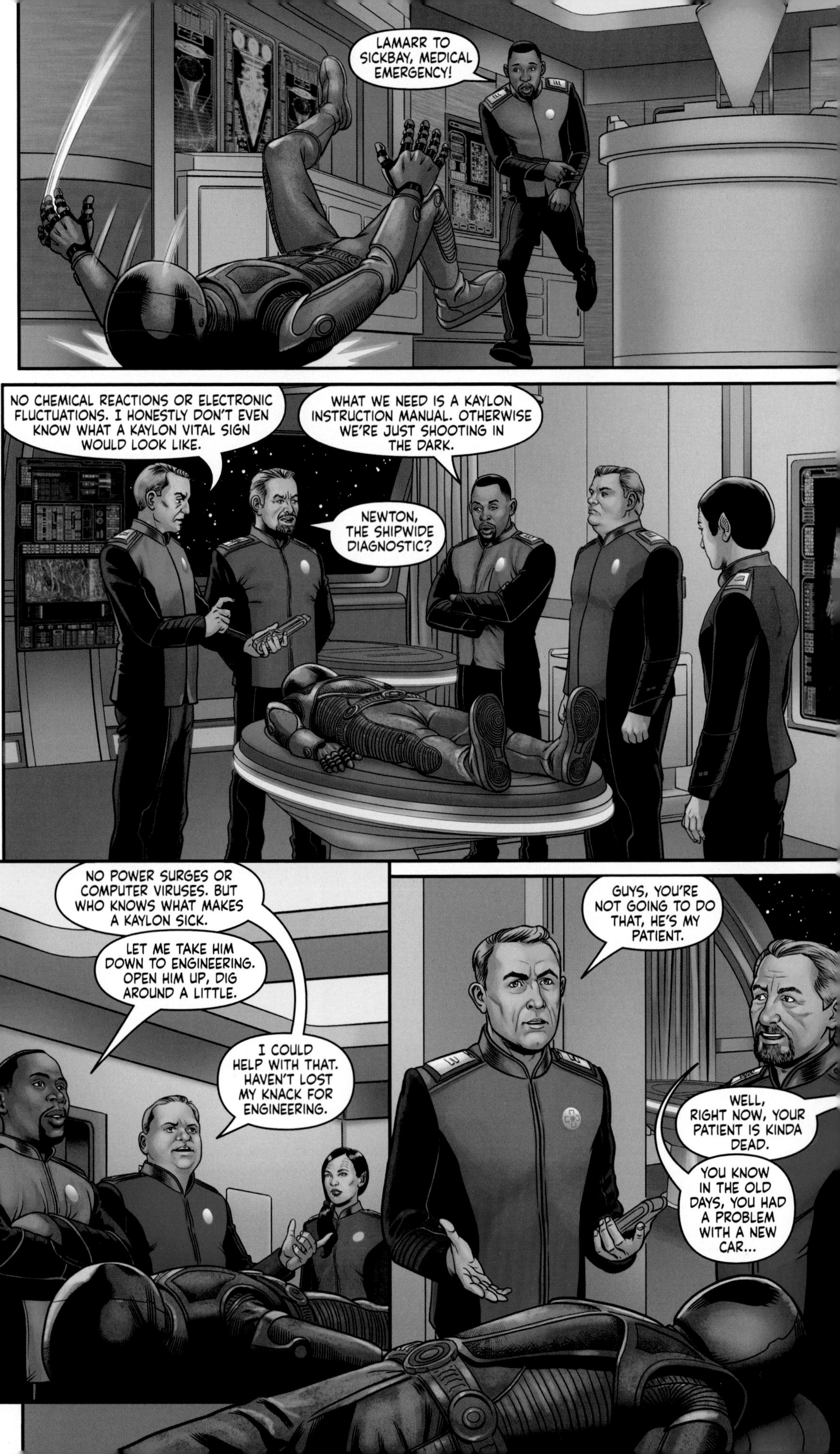
LAMARR TO SICKBAY, MEDICAL EMERGENCY!
NO CHEMICAL REACTIONS OR ELECTRONIC FLUCTUATIONS. I HONESTLY DON'T EVEN KNOW WHAT A KAYLON VITAL SIGN WOULD LOOK LIKE.
WHAT WE NEED IS A KAYLON INSTRUCTION MANUAL. OTHERWISE WE'RE JUST SHOOTING IN THE DARK.
NEWTON, THE SHIPWIDE DIAGNOSTIC?
NO POWER SURGES OR COMPUTER VIRUSES. BUT WHO KNOWS WHAT MAKES A KAYLON SICK.
LET ME TAKE HIM DOWN TO ENGINEERING. OPEN HIM UP, DIG AROUND A LITTLE.
I COULD HELP WITH THAT. HAVEN'T LOST MY KNACK FOR ENGINEERING.
GUYS, YOU'RE NOT GOING TO DO THAT, HE'S MY PATIENT.
WELL, RIGHT NOW, YOUR PATIENT IS KINDA DEAD.
YOU KNOW IN THE OLD DAYS, YOU HAD A PROBLEM WITH A NEW CAR...

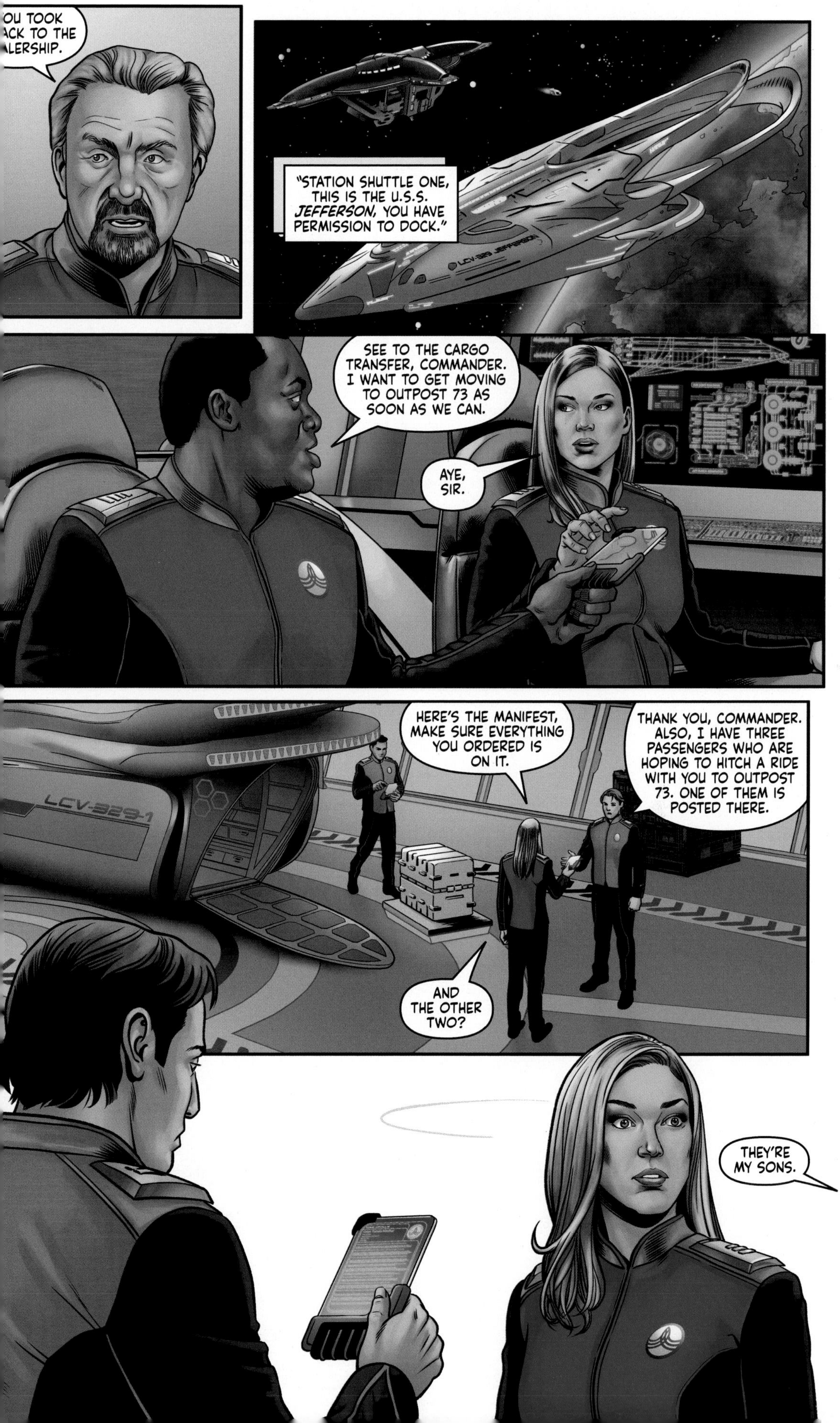
OU TOOK ACK TO THE ALERSHIP.
"STATION SHUTTLE ONE, THIS IS THE U.S.S. *JEFFERSON,* YOU HAVE PERMISSION TO DOCK."
SEE TO THE CARGO TRANSFER, COMMANDER. I WANT TO GET MOVING TO OUTPOST 73 AS SOON AS WE CAN.
AYE, SIR.
HERE'S THE MANIFEST, MAKE SURE EVERYTHING YOU ORDERED IS ON IT.
THANK YOU, COMMANDER. ALSO, I HAVE THREE PASSENGERS WHO ARE HOPING TO HITCH A RIDE WITH YOU TO OUTPOST 73. ONE OF THEM IS POSTED THERE.
AND THE OTHER TWO?
THEY'RE MY SONS.

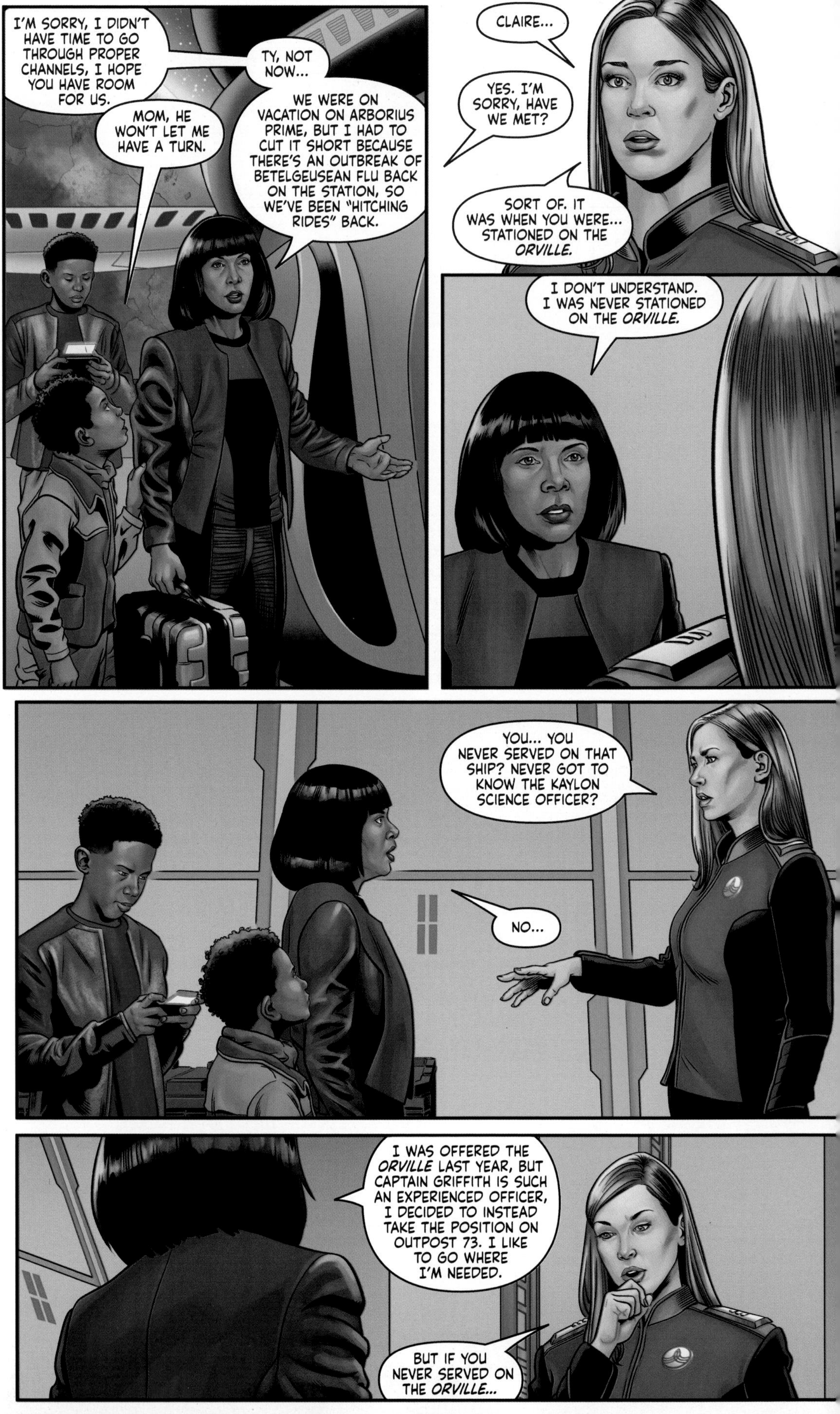
I'M SORRY, I DIDN'T HAVE TIME TO GO THROUGH PROPER CHANNELS, I HOPE YOU HAVE ROOM FOR US.
TY, NOT NOW...
MOM, HE WON'T LET ME HAVE A TURN.
WE WERE ON VACATION ON ARBORIUS PRIME, BUT I HAD TO CUT IT SHORT BECAUSE THERE'S AN OUTBREAK OF BETELGEUSEAN FLU BACK ON THE STATION, SO WE'VE BEEN "HITCHING RIDES" BACK.
CLAIRE...
YES. I'M SORRY, HAVE WE MET?
SORT OF. IT WAS WHEN YOU WERE... STATIONED ON THE *ORVILLE.*
I DON'T UNDERSTAND. I WAS NEVER STATIONED ON THE *ORVILLE.*
YOU... YOU NEVER SERVED ON THAT SHIP? NEVER GOT TO KNOW THE KAYLON SCIENCE OFFICER?
NO...
I WAS OFFERED THE *ORVILLE* LAST YEAR, BUT CAPTAIN GRIFFITH IS SUCH AN EXPERIENCED OFFICER, I DECIDED TO INSTEAD TAKE THE POSITION ON OUTPOST 73. I LIKE TO GO WHERE I'M NEEDED.
BUT IF YOU NEVER SERVED ON THE *ORVILLE*...

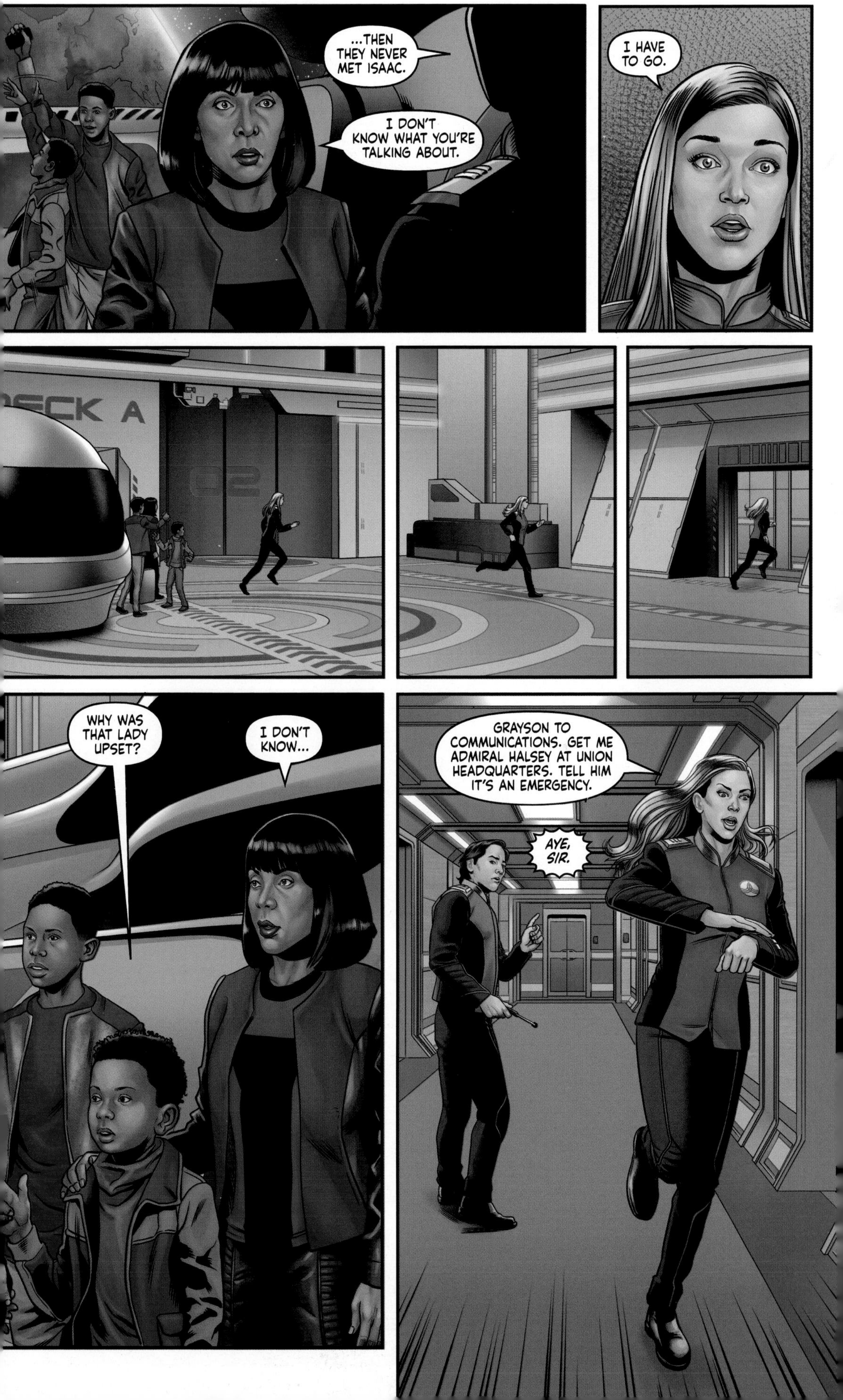
...THEN THEY NEVER MET ISAAC.
I DON'T KNOW WHAT YOU'RE TALKING ABOUT.
I HAVE TO GO.
WHY WAS THAT LADY UPSET?
I DON'T KNOW...
GRAYSON TO COMMUNICATIONS. GET ME ADMIRAL HALSEY AT UNION HEADQUARTERS. TELL HIM IT'S AN EMERGENCY.
AYE, SIR.

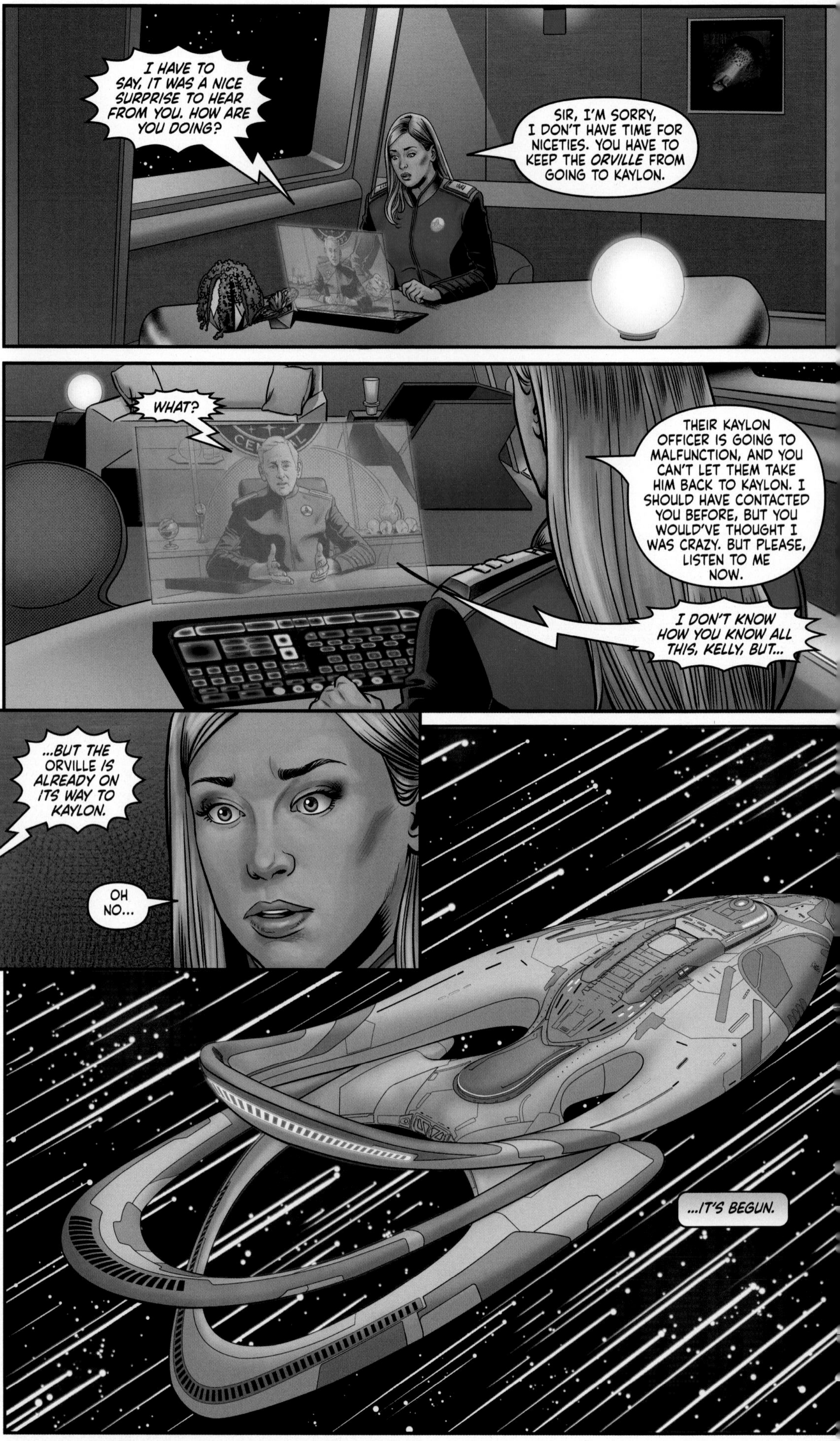
I HAVE TO SAY, IT WAS A NICE SURPRISE TO HEAR FROM YOU. HOW ARE YOU DOING?
SIR, I'M SORRY, I DON'T HAVE TIME FOR NICETIES. YOU HAVE TO KEEP THE ORVILLE FROM GOING TO KAYLON.
WHAT?
THEIR KAYLON OFFICER IS GOING TO MALFUNCTION, AND YOU CAN'T LET THEM TAKE HIM BACK TO KAYLON. I SHOULD HAVE CONTACTED YOU BEFORE, BUT YOU WOULD'VE THOUGHT I WAS CRAZY. BUT PLEASE, LISTEN TO ME NOW.
I DON'T KNOW HOW YOU KNOW ALL THIS, KELLY, BUT...
...BUT THE ORVILLE IS ALREADY ON ITS WAY TO KAYLON.
OH NO...
...IT'S BEGUN.

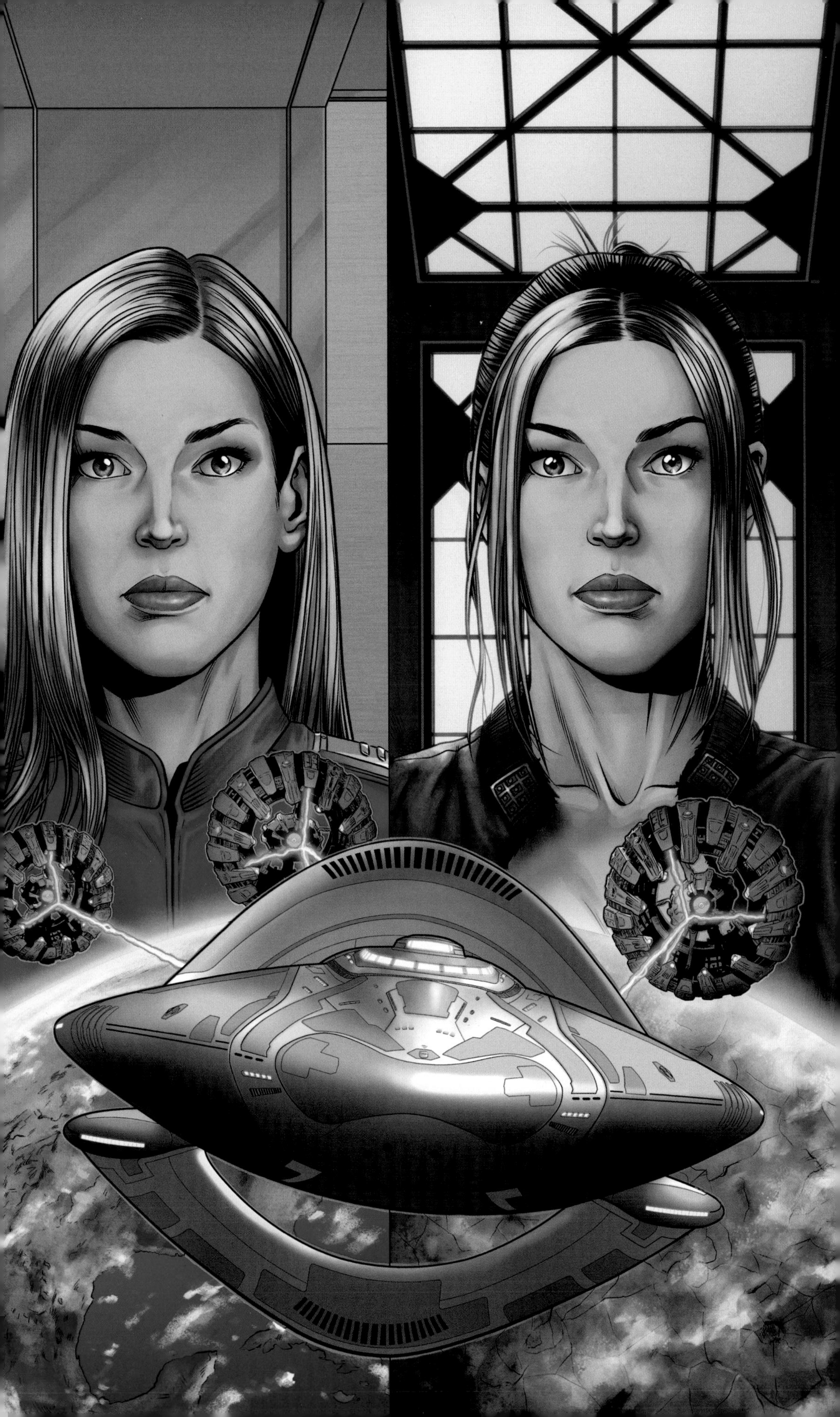

DIGRESSIONS PART 2

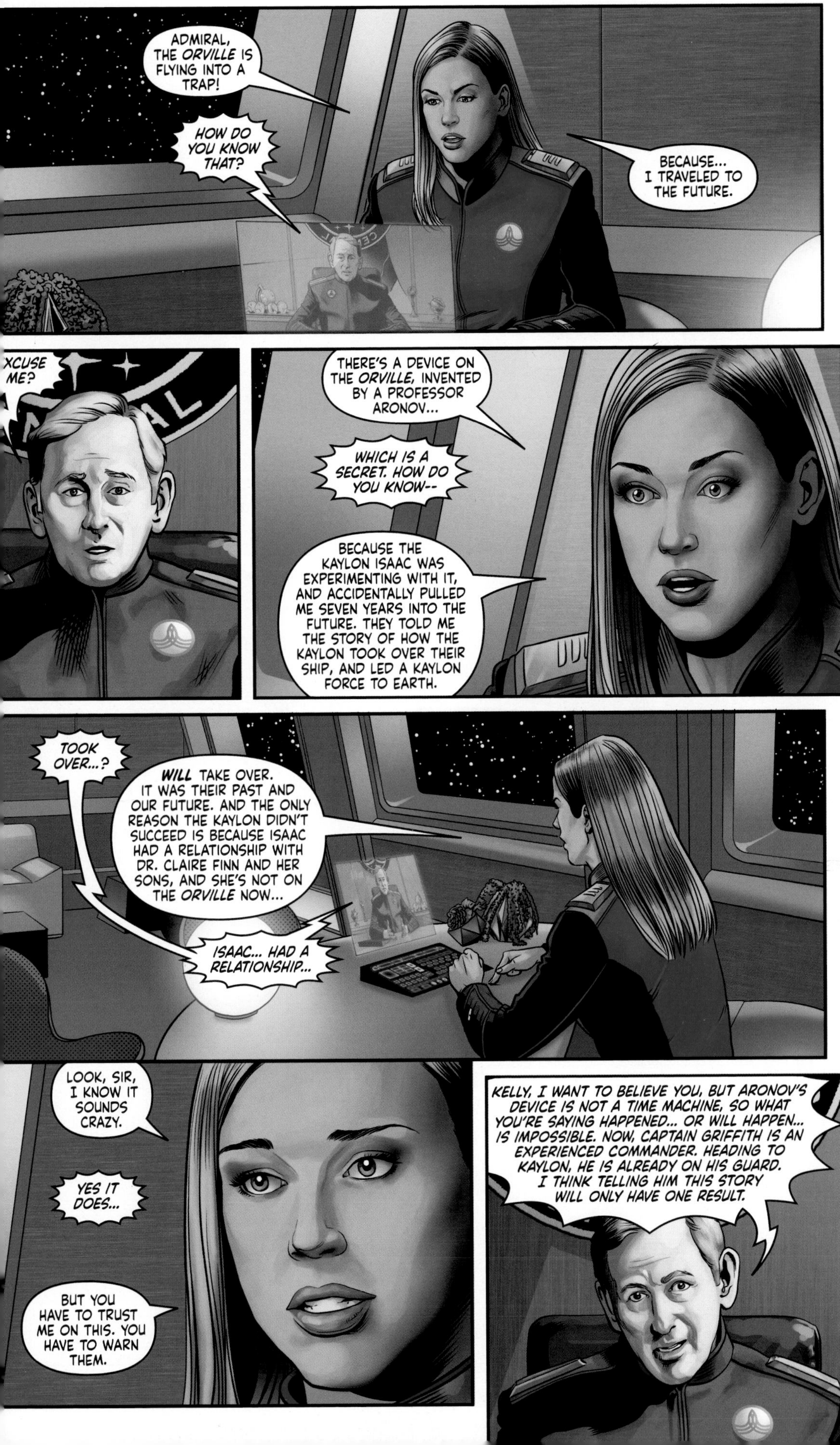
ADMIRAL, THE *ORVILLE* IS FLYING INTO A TRAP!
HOW DO YOU KNOW THAT?
BECAUSE... I TRAVELED TO THE FUTURE.
XCUSE ME?
THERE'S A DEVICE ON THE *ORVILLE*, INVENTED BY A PROFESSOR ARONOV...
WHICH IS A SECRET. HOW DO YOU KNOW--
BECAUSE THE KAYLON ISAAC WAS EXPERIMENTING WITH IT, AND ACCIDENTALLY PULLED ME SEVEN YEARS INTO THE FUTURE. THEY TOLD ME THE STORY OF HOW THE KAYLON TOOK OVER THEIR SHIP, AND LED A KAYLON FORCE TO EARTH.
TOOK OVER...?
WILL TAKE OVER. IT WAS THEIR PAST AND OUR FUTURE. AND THE ONLY REASON THE KAYLON DIDN'T SUCCEED IS BECAUSE ISAAC HAD A RELATIONSHIP WITH DR. CLAIRE FINN AND HER SONS, AND SHE'S NOT ON THE *ORVILLE* NOW...
ISAAC... HAD A RELATIONSHIP...
LOOK, SIR, I KNOW IT SOUNDS CRAZY.
YES IT DOES...
BUT YOU HAVE TO TRUST ME ON THIS. YOU HAVE TO WARN THEM.
KELLY, I WANT TO BELIEVE YOU, BUT ARONOV'S DEVICE IS NOT A TIME MACHINE, SO WHAT YOU'RE SAYING HAPPENED... OR WILL HAPPEN... IS IMPOSSIBLE. NOW, CAPTAIN GRIFFITH IS AN EXPERIENCED COMMANDER. HEADING TO KAYLON, HE IS ALREADY ON HIS GUARD. I THINK TELLING HIM THIS STORY WILL ONLY HAVE ONE RESULT.

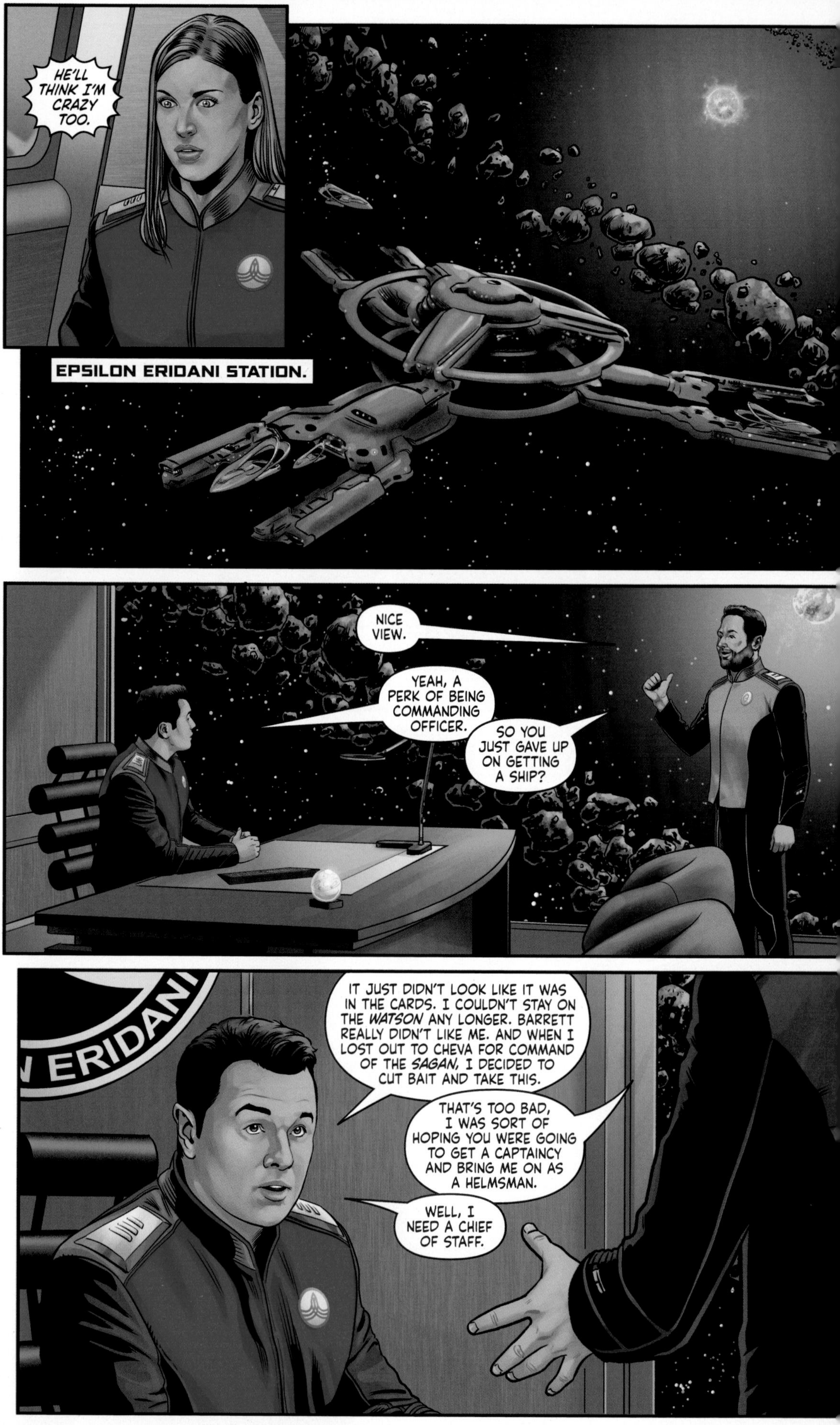
HE'LL THINK I'M CRAZY TOO.
EPSILON ERIDANI STATION.
NICE VIEW.
YEAH, A PERK OF BEING COMMANDING OFFICER.
SO YOU JUST GAVE UP ON GETTING A SHIP?
ERIDANI
IT JUST DIDN'T LOOK LIKE IT WAS IN THE CARDS. I COULDN'T STAY ON THE *WATSON* ANY LONGER. BARRETT REALLY DIDN'T LIKE ME. AND WHEN I LOST OUT TO CHEVA FOR COMMAND OF THE *SAGAN*, I DECIDED TO CUT BAIT AND TAKE THIS.
THAT'S TOO BAD, I WAS SORT OF HOPING YOU WERE GOING TO GET A CAPTAINCY AND BRING ME ON AS A HELMSMAN.
WELL, I NEED A CHIEF OF STAFF.

YOU WANT ME TO RECOMMEND SOMEBODY?

NO, IDIOT, I WANT YOU TO BE MY CHIEF OF STAFF.

SERIOUSLY?

HEY, THANKS. WHAT'S A CHIEF OF STAFF DO?

NO IDEA. BUT PROBABLY NOT A LOT TO WORRY ABOUT. NOT LIKE ANYTHING IMPORTANT'S GOING ON.

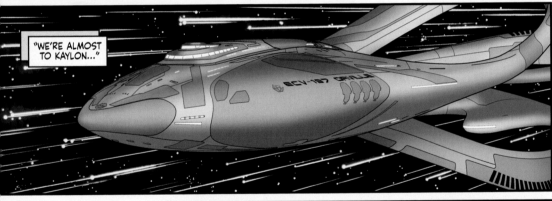

"WE'RE ALMOST TO KAYLON..."

ECV-197 ORVILLE

...AND NO CHANGE IN ISAAC. I HOPE IT WON'T BE TOO LATE FOR HIS PEOPLE TO FIX HIM.

UNLESS THEY JUST WANT TO USE HIM FOR PARTS. WHO KNOWS WHAT KAYLON DO WITH THEIR DEAD?

CAPTAIN...

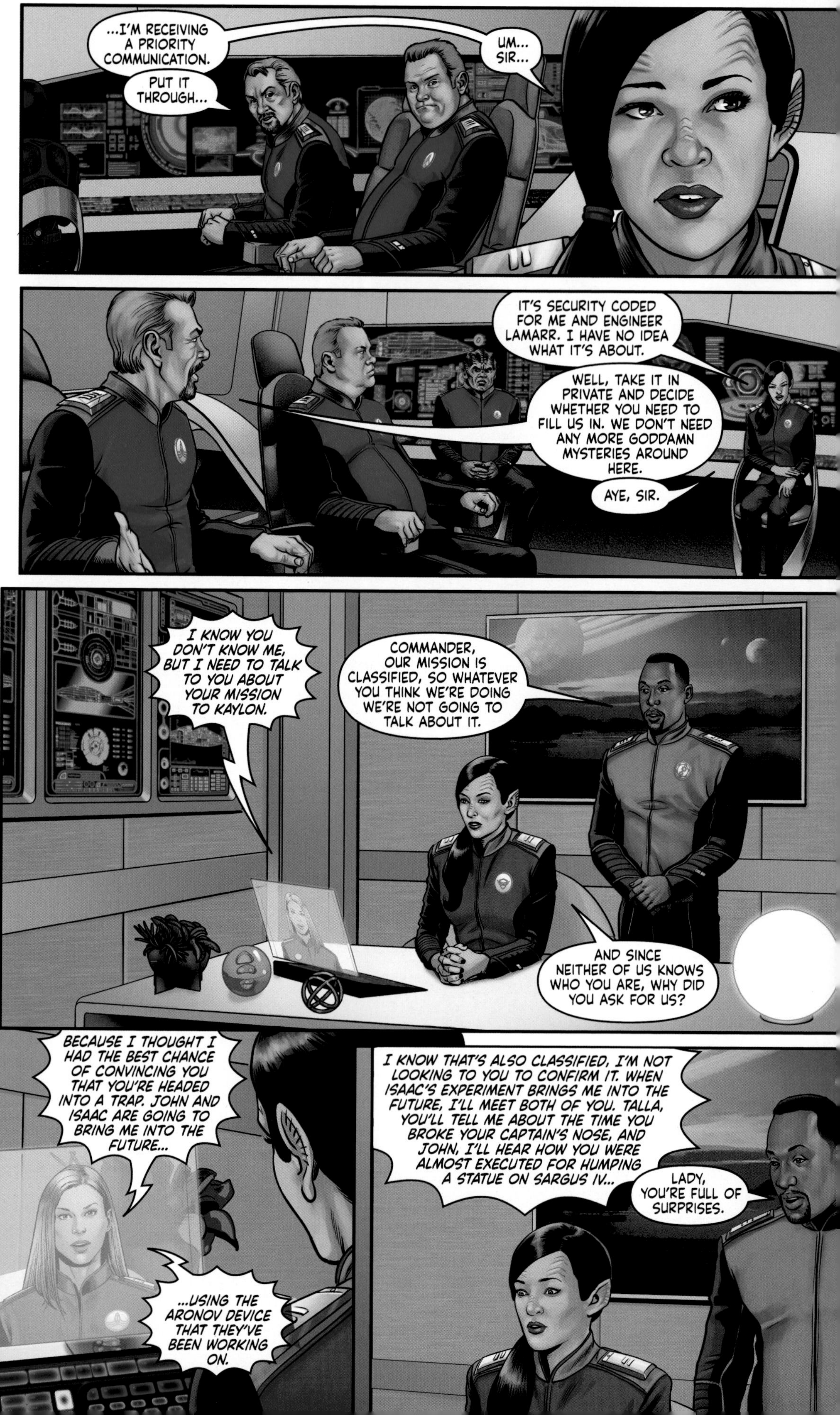
...I'M RECEIVING A PRIORITY COMMUNICATION.
PUT IT THROUGH...
UM... SIR...
IT'S SECURITY CODED FOR ME AND ENGINEER LAMARR. I HAVE NO IDEA WHAT IT'S ABOUT.
WELL, TAKE IT IN PRIVATE AND DECIDE WHETHER YOU NEED TO FILL US IN. WE DON'T NEED ANY MORE GODDAMN MYSTERIES AROUND HERE.
AYE, SIR.
I KNOW YOU DON'T KNOW ME, BUT I NEED TO TALK TO YOU ABOUT YOUR MISSION TO KAYLON.
COMMANDER, OUR MISSION IS CLASSIFIED, SO WHATEVER YOU THINK WE'RE DOING WE'RE NOT GOING TO TALK ABOUT IT.
AND SINCE NEITHER OF US KNOWS WHO YOU ARE, WHY DID YOU ASK FOR US?
BECAUSE I THOUGHT I HAD THE BEST CHANCE OF CONVINCING YOU THAT YOU'RE HEADED INTO A TRAP. JOHN AND ISAAC ARE GOING TO BRING ME INTO THE FUTURE...
...USING THE ARONOV DEVICE THAT THEY'VE BEEN WORKING ON.
I KNOW THAT'S ALSO CLASSIFIED, I'M NOT LOOKING TO YOU TO CONFIRM IT. WHEN ISAAC'S EXPERIMENT BRINGS ME INTO THE FUTURE, I'LL MEET BOTH OF YOU. TALLA, YOU'LL TELL ME ABOUT THE TIME YOU BROKE YOUR CAPTAIN'S NOSE, AND JOHN, I'LL HEAR HOW YOU WERE ALMOST EXECUTED FOR HUMPING A STATUE ON SARGUS IV...
LADY, YOU'RE FULL OF SURPRISES.

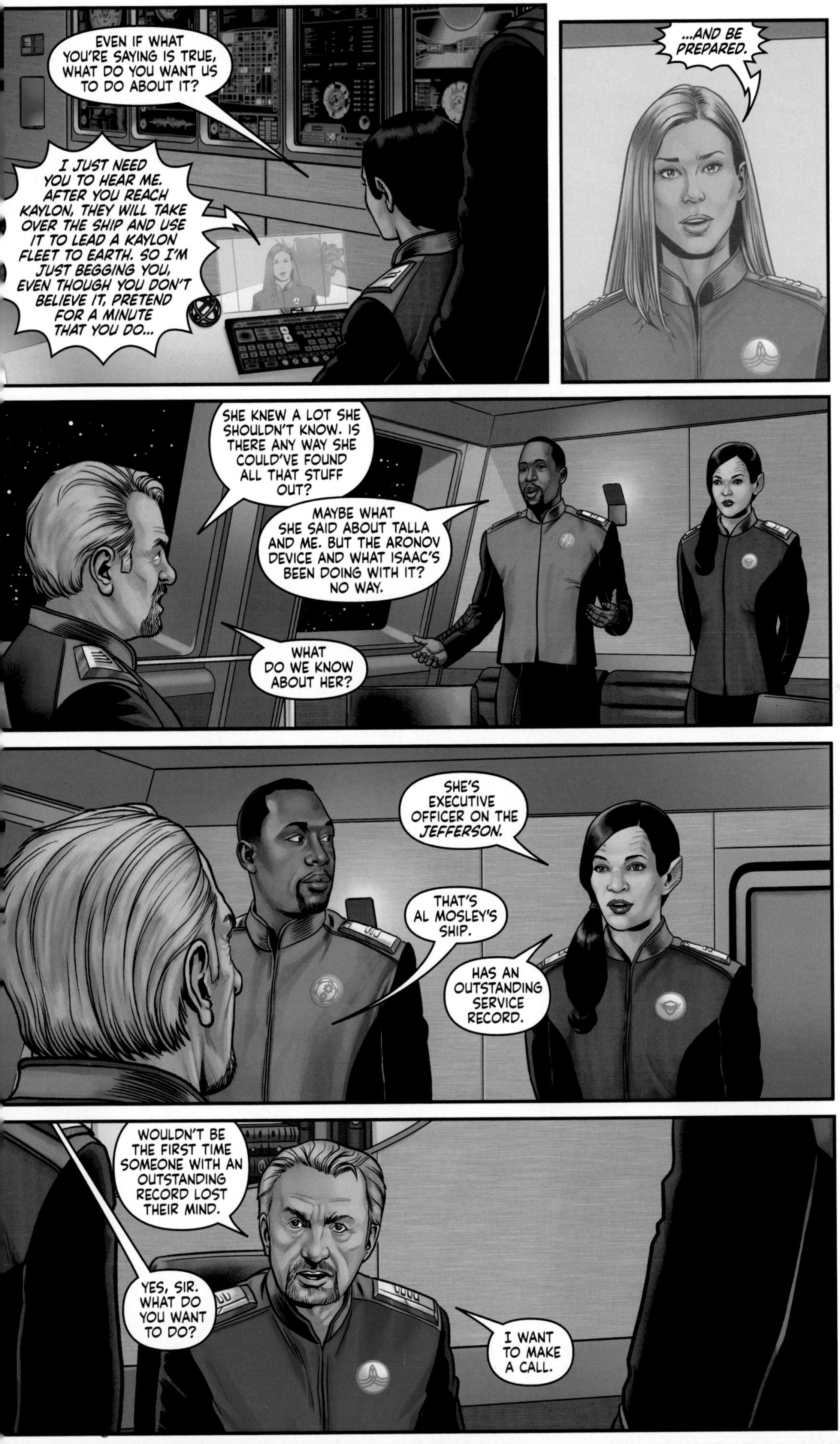
EVEN IF WHAT YOU'RE SAYING IS TRUE, WHAT DO YOU WANT US TO DO ABOUT IT?
I JUST NEED YOU TO HEAR ME. AFTER YOU REACH KAYLON, THEY WILL TAKE OVER THE SHIP AND USE IT TO LEAD A KAYLON FLEET TO EARTH. SO I'M JUST BEGGING YOU, EVEN THOUGH YOU DON'T BELIEVE IT, PRETEND FOR A MINUTE THAT YOU DO...
...AND BE PREPARED.
SHE KNEW A LOT SHE SHOULDN'T KNOW. IS THERE ANY WAY SHE COULD'VE FOUND ALL THAT STUFF OUT?
MAYBE WHAT SHE SAID ABOUT TALLA AND ME. BUT THE ARONOV DEVICE AND WHAT ISAAC'S BEEN DOING WITH IT? NO WAY.
WHAT DO WE KNOW ABOUT HER?
SHE'S EXECUTIVE OFFICER ON THE *JEFFERSON.*
THAT'S AL MOSLEY'S SHIP.
HAS AN OUTSTANDING SERVICE RECORD.
WOULDN'T BE THE FIRST TIME SOMEONE WITH AN OUTSTANDING RECORD LOST THEIR MIND.
YES, SIR. WHAT DO YOU WANT TO DO?
I WANT TO MAKE A CALL.

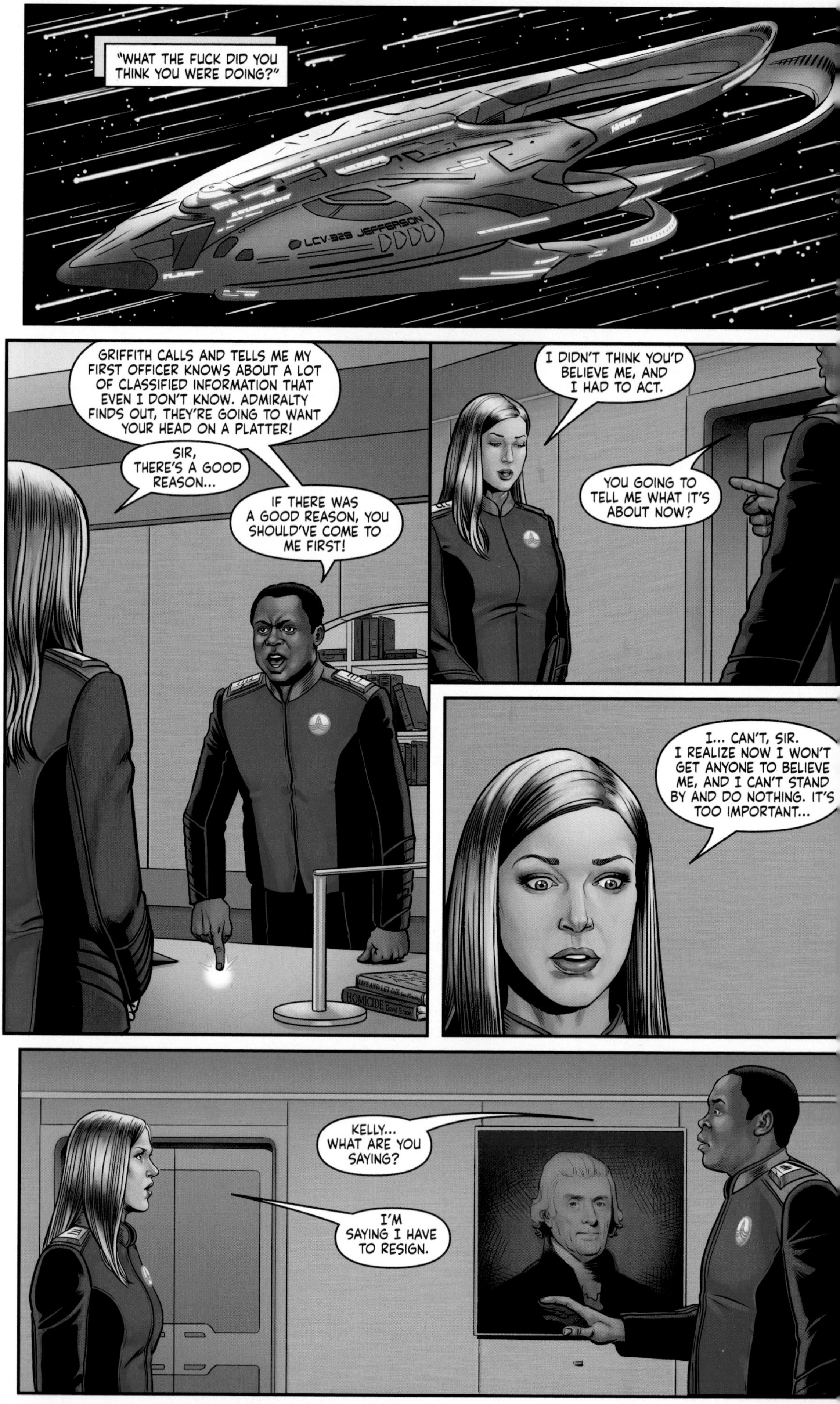
"WHAT THE FUCK DID YOU THINK YOU WERE DOING?"
LCV-329 JEFFERSON
GRIFFITH CALLS AND TELLS ME MY FIRST OFFICER KNOWS ABOUT A LOT OF CLASSIFIED INFORMATION THAT EVEN I DON'T KNOW. ADMIRALTY FINDS OUT, THEY'RE GOING TO WANT YOUR HEAD ON A PLATTER!
SIR, THERE'S A GOOD REASON...
IF THERE WAS A GOOD REASON, YOU SHOULD'VE COME TO ME FIRST!
I DIDN'T THINK YOU'D BELIEVE ME, AND I HAD TO ACT.
YOU GOING TO TELL ME WHAT IT'S ABOUT NOW?
I... CAN'T, SIR. I REALIZE NOW I WON'T GET ANYONE TO BELIEVE ME, AND I CAN'T STAND BY AND DO NOTHING. IT'S TOO IMPORTANT...
KELLY... WHAT ARE YOU SAYING?
I'M SAYING I HAVE TO RESIGN.

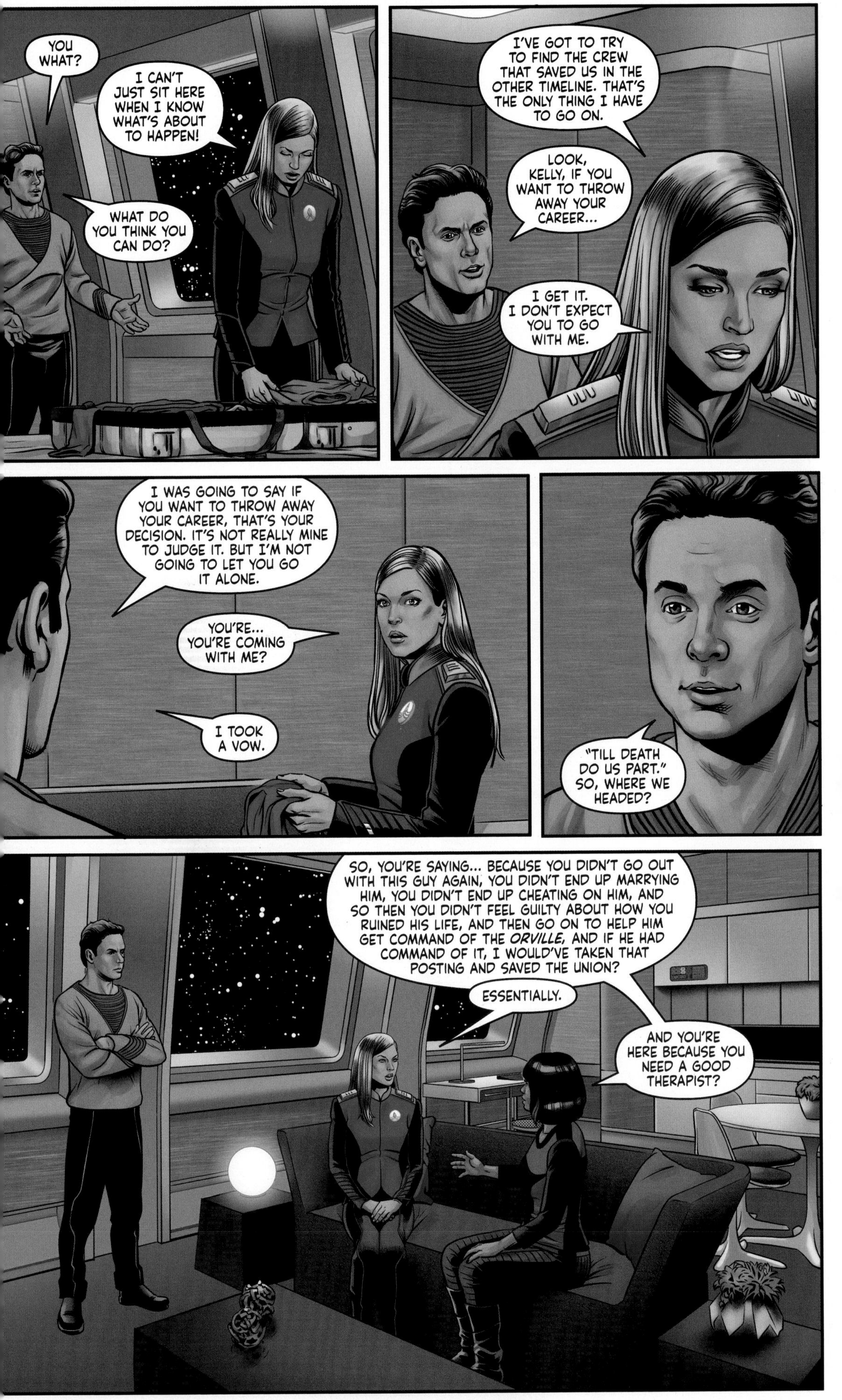
YOU WHAT?
I CAN'T JUST SIT HERE WHEN I KNOW WHAT'S ABOUT TO HAPPEN!
WHAT DO YOU THINK YOU CAN DO?
I'VE GOT TO TRY TO FIND THE CREW THAT SAVED US IN THE OTHER TIMELINE. THAT'S THE ONLY THING I HAVE TO GO ON.
LOOK, KELLY, IF YOU WANT TO THROW AWAY YOUR CAREER...
I GET IT. I DON'T EXPECT YOU TO GO WITH ME.
I WAS GOING TO SAY IF YOU WANT TO THROW AWAY YOUR CAREER, THAT'S YOUR DECISION. IT'S NOT REALLY MINE TO JUDGE IT. BUT I'M NOT GOING TO LET YOU GO IT ALONE.
YOU'RE... YOU'RE COMING WITH ME?
I TOOK A VOW.
"TILL DEATH DO US PART." SO, WHERE WE HEADED?
SO, YOU'RE SAYING... BECAUSE YOU DIDN'T GO OUT WITH THIS GUY AGAIN, YOU DIDN'T END UP MARRYING HIM, YOU DIDN'T END UP CHEATING ON HIM, AND SO THEN YOU DIDN'T FEEL GUILTY ABOUT HOW YOU RUINED HIS LIFE, AND THEN GO ON TO HELP HIM GET COMMAND OF THE *ORVILLE*, AND IF HE HAD COMMAND OF IT, I WOULD'VE TAKEN THAT POSTING AND SAVED THE UNION?
ESSENTIALLY.
AND YOU'RE HERE BECAUSE YOU NEED A GOOD THERAPIST?

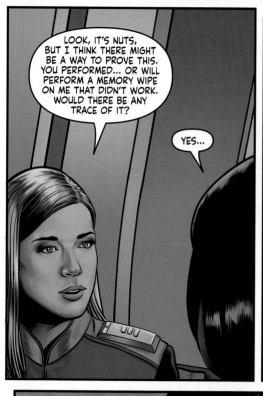

LOOK, IT'S NUTS, BUT I THINK THERE MIGHT BE A WAY TO PROVE THIS. YOU PERFORMED... OR WILL PERFORM A MEMORY WIPE ON ME THAT DIDN'T WORK. WOULD THERE BE ANY TRACE OF IT?

YES...

WELL, THERE IS EVIDENCE THAT SOMEONE TRIED TO PERFORM A MEMORY WIPE ON YOU.

IS THERE A REASON IT DIDN'T WORK?

HER BRAIN IS DEFICIENT IN A PROTEIN CALLED BETA-SECRETASE. A DOCTOR PERFORMING THE MEMORY WIPE MIGHT HAVE MISSED THAT IF THEY WEREN'T LOOKING FOR IT.

THE QUESTION IS, WOULD *YOU* HAVE MISSED IT?

EASILY.

SO, WHERE ARE WE HEADED?

WELL, WE'LL BE AT OUTPOST 73 IN A FEW DAYS. WE'LL HAVE TO GET OTHER TRANSPORTATION. I JUST HOPE WE'RE NOT TOO LATE.

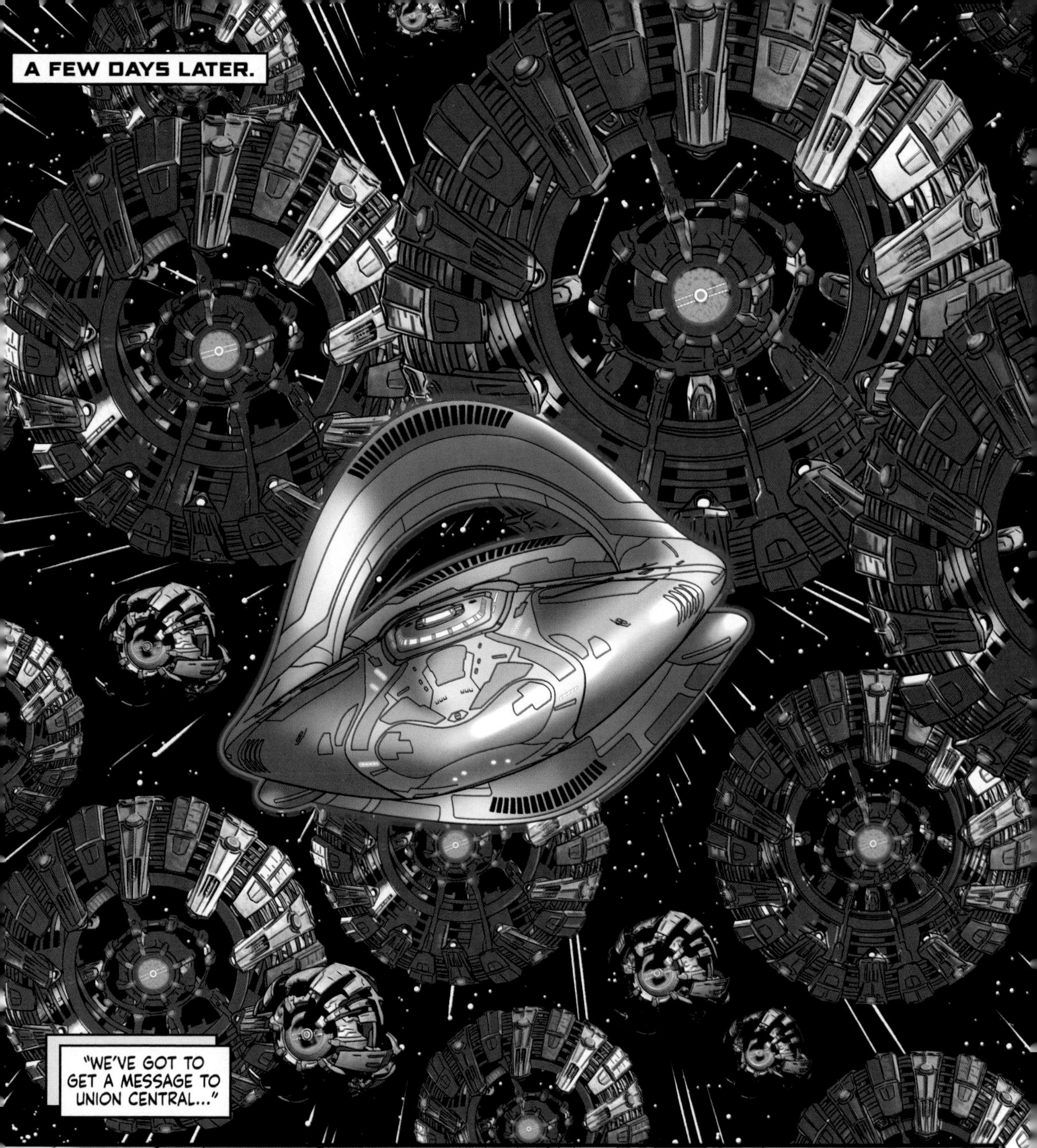
A FEW DAYS LATER.
"WE'VE GOT TO GET A MESSAGE TO UNION CENTRAL..."

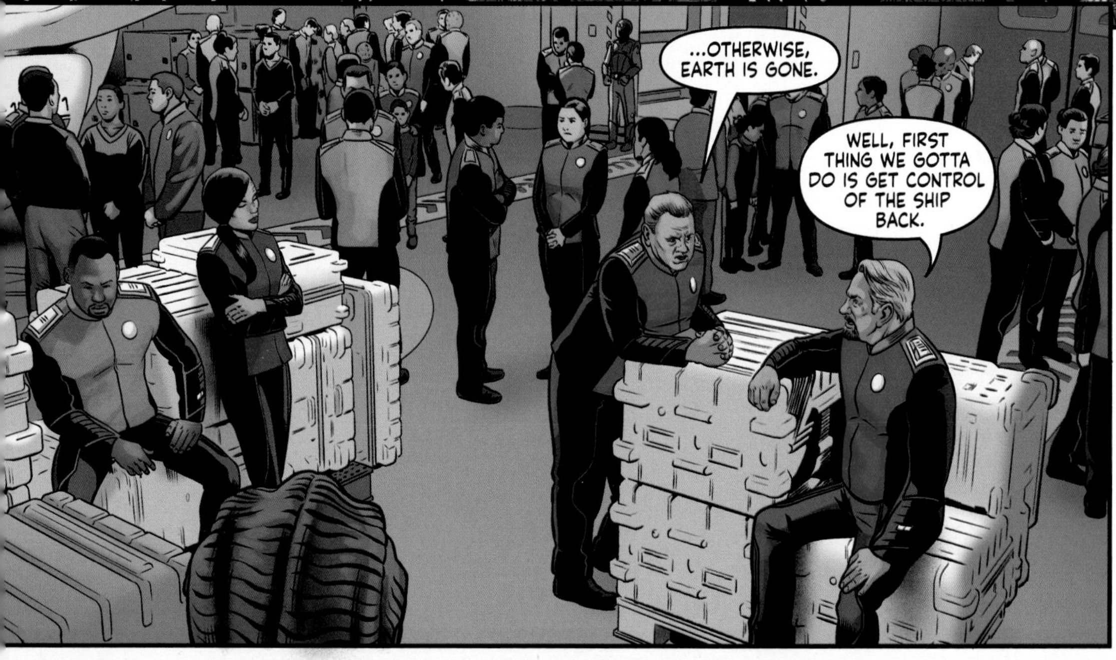
...OTHERWISE, EARTH IS GONE.
WELL, FIRST THING WE GOTTA DO IS GET CONTROL OF THE SHIP BACK.

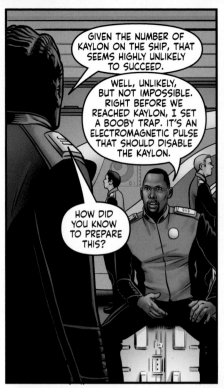

GIVEN THE NUMBER OF KAYLON ON THE SHIP, THAT SEEMS HIGHLY UNLIKELY TO SUCCEED.

WELL, UNLIKELY, BUT NOT IMPOSSIBLE. RIGHT BEFORE WE REACHED KAYLON, I SET A BOOBY TRAP. IT'S AN ELECTROMAGNETIC PULSE THAT SHOULD DISABLE THE KAYLON.

HOW DID YOU KNOW TO PREPARE THIS?

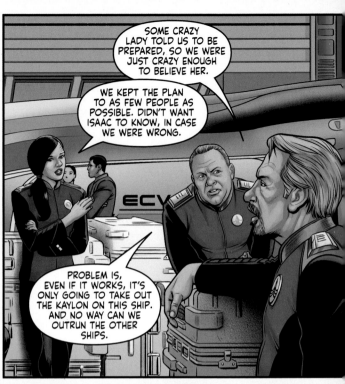

SOME CRAZY LADY TOLD US TO BE PREPARED, SO WE WERE JUST CRAZY ENOUGH TO BELIEVE HER.

WE KEPT THE PLAN TO AS FEW PEOPLE AS POSSIBLE. DIDN'T WANT ISAAC TO KNOW, IN CASE WE WERE WRONG.

PROBLEM IS, EVEN IF IT WORKS, IT'S ONLY GOING TO TAKE OUT THE KAYLON ON THIS SHIP. AND NO WAY CAN WE OUTRUN THE OTHER SHIPS.

WE'LL TAKE CONTROL OF THE SHIP NEAR EARTH, GET A MESSAGE OUT THEN. HOPEFULLY WE CAN HOLD THEM OFF UNTIL HELP ARRIVES.

JUST US?

NO CHOICE. WE TAKE CONTROL OF THE SHIP TOO SOON, THE KAYLON WILL BE ONTO US AND WE'LL BE DESTROYED, AND WE WON'T DO ANYBODY ANY GOOD.

WE WILL PREVAIL.

OUTPOST 73.

"MOM, THIS SHIP SMELLS."

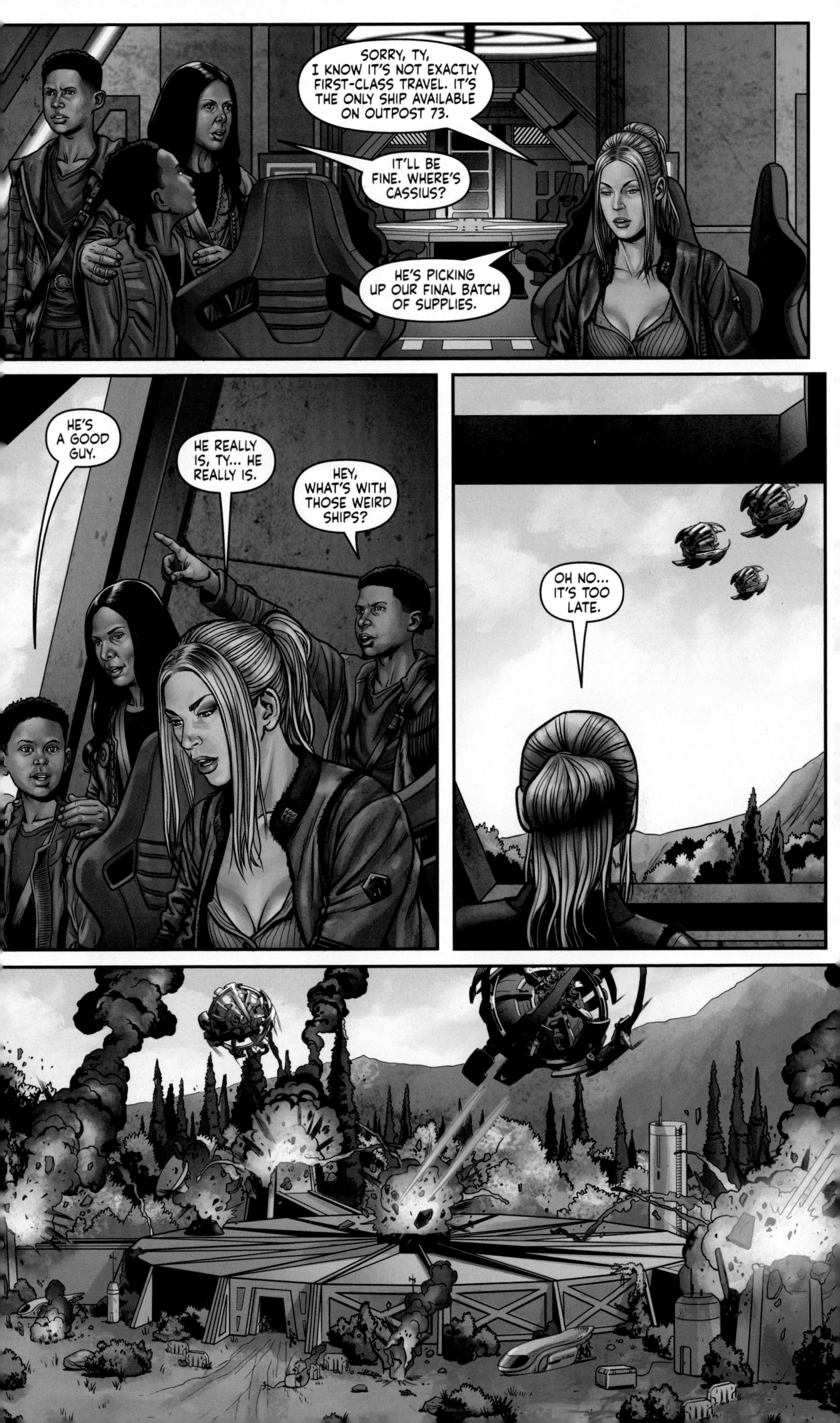
SORRY, TY, I KNOW IT'S NOT EXACTLY FIRST-CLASS TRAVEL. IT'S THE ONLY SHIP AVAILABLE ON OUTPOST 73.
IT'LL BE FINE. WHERE'S CASSIUS?
HE'S PICKING UP OUR FINAL BATCH OF SUPPLIES.
HE'S A GOOD GUY.
HE REALLY IS, TY... HE REALLY IS.
HEY, WHAT'S WITH THOSE WEIRD SHIPS?
OH NO... IT'S TOO LATE.

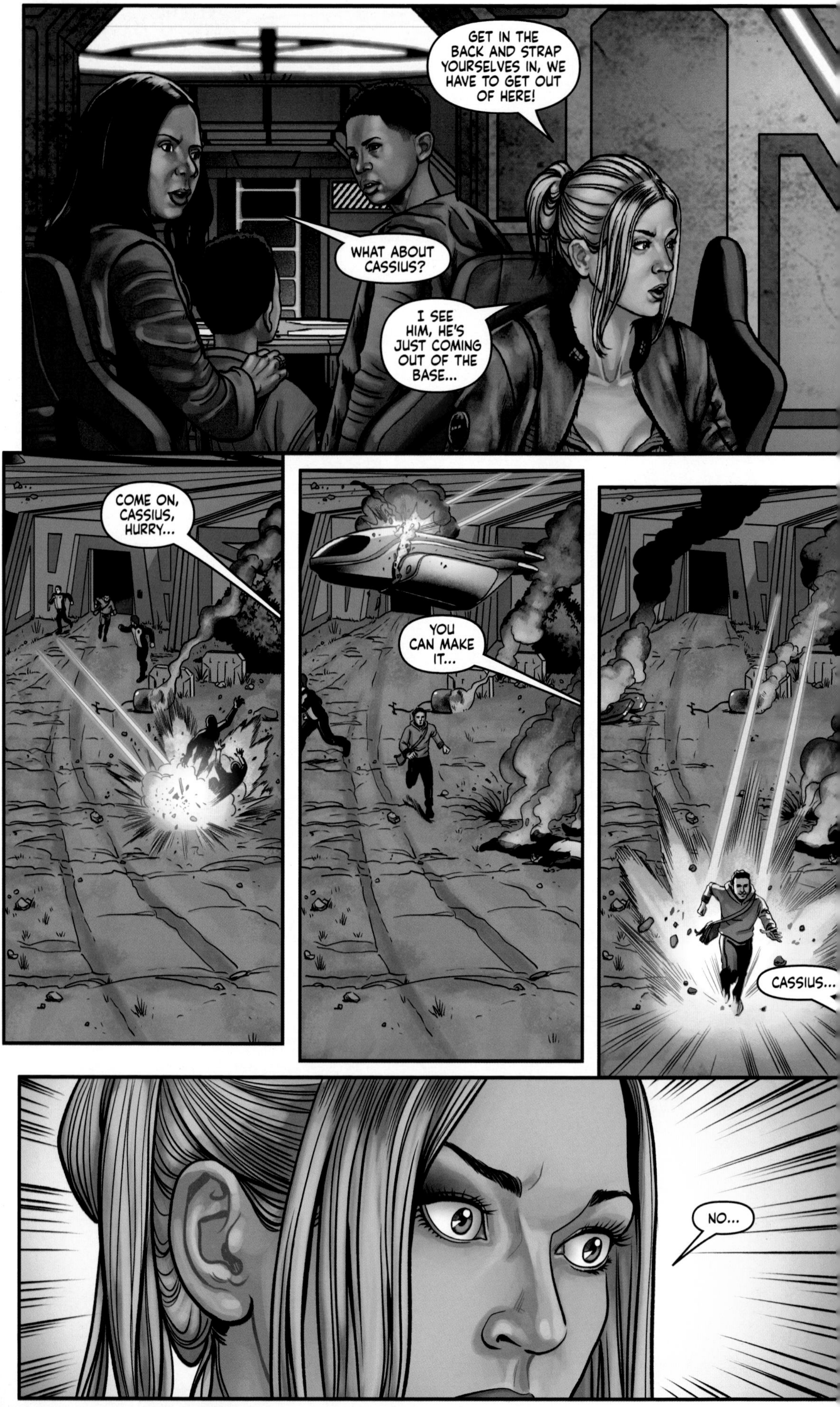
GET IN THE BACK AND STRAP YOURSELVES IN, WE HAVE TO GET OUT OF HERE!
WHAT ABOUT CASSIUS?
I SEE HIM, HE'S JUST COMING OUT OF THE BASE...
COME ON, CASSIUS, HURRY...
YOU CAN MAKE IT...
CASSIUS...
NO...

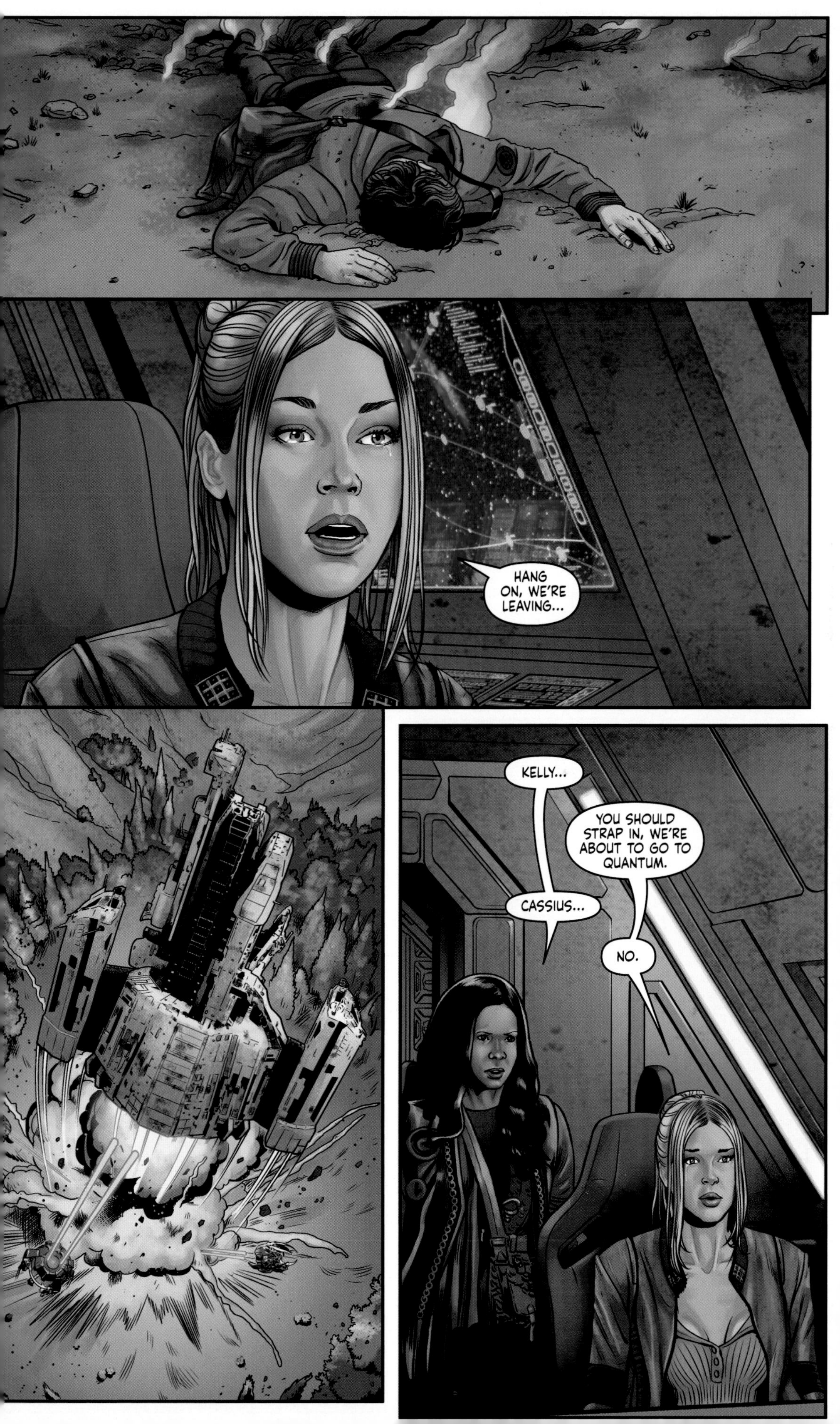

HANG ON, WE'RE LEAVING...
KELLY...
CASSIUS...
YOU SHOULD STRAP IN, WE'RE ABOUT TO GO TO QUANTUM.
NO.

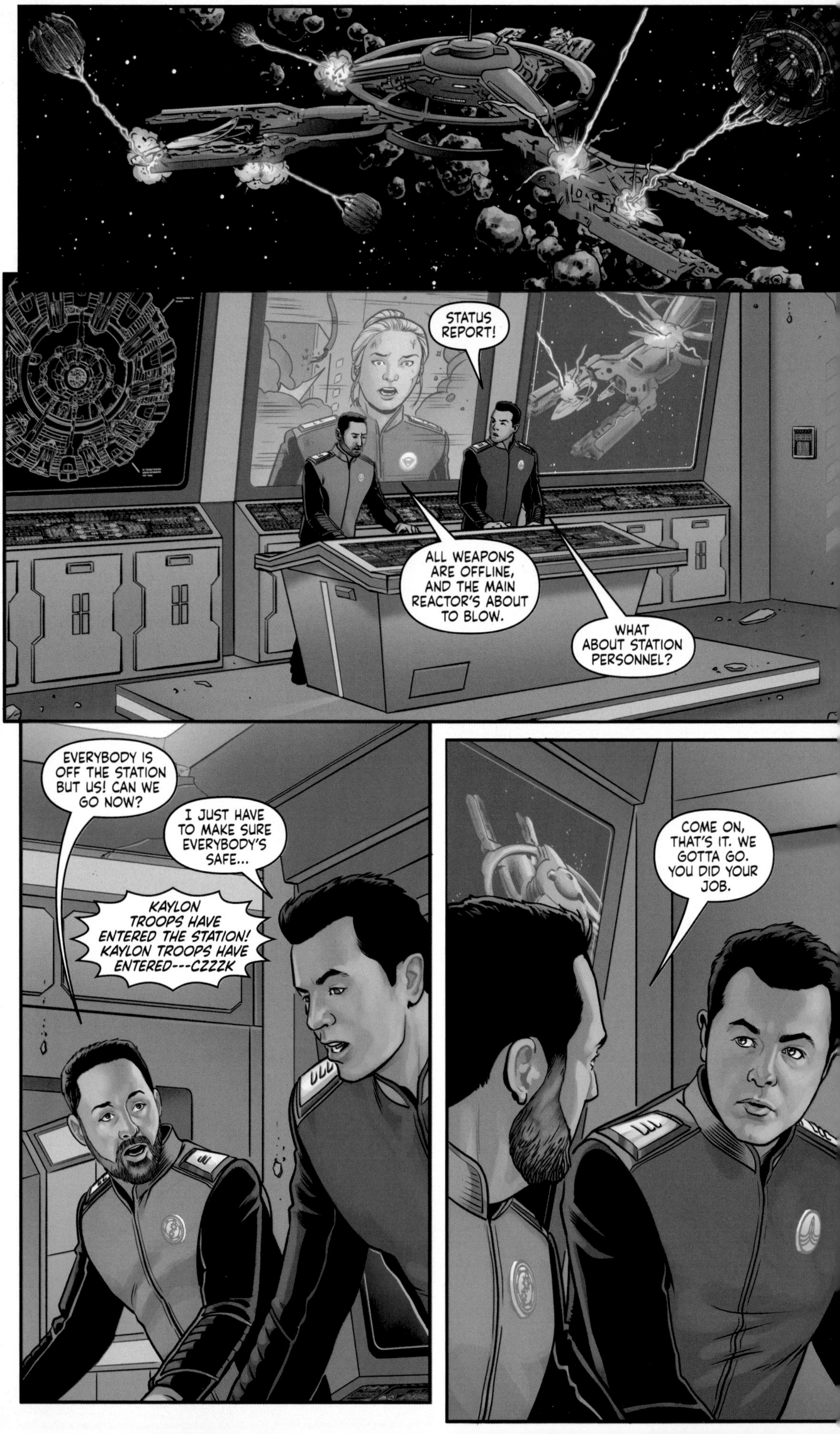

STATUS REPORT!
ALL WEAPONS ARE OFFLINE, AND THE MAIN REACTOR'S ABOUT TO BLOW.
WHAT ABOUT STATION PERSONNEL?
EVERYBODY IS OFF THE STATION BUT US! CAN WE GO NOW?
I JUST HAVE TO MAKE SURE EVERYBODY'S SAFE...
KAYLON TROOPS HAVE ENTERED THE STATION! KAYLON TROOPS HAVE ENTERED---CZZZK
COME ON, THAT'S IT. WE GOTTA GO. YOU DID YOUR JOB.

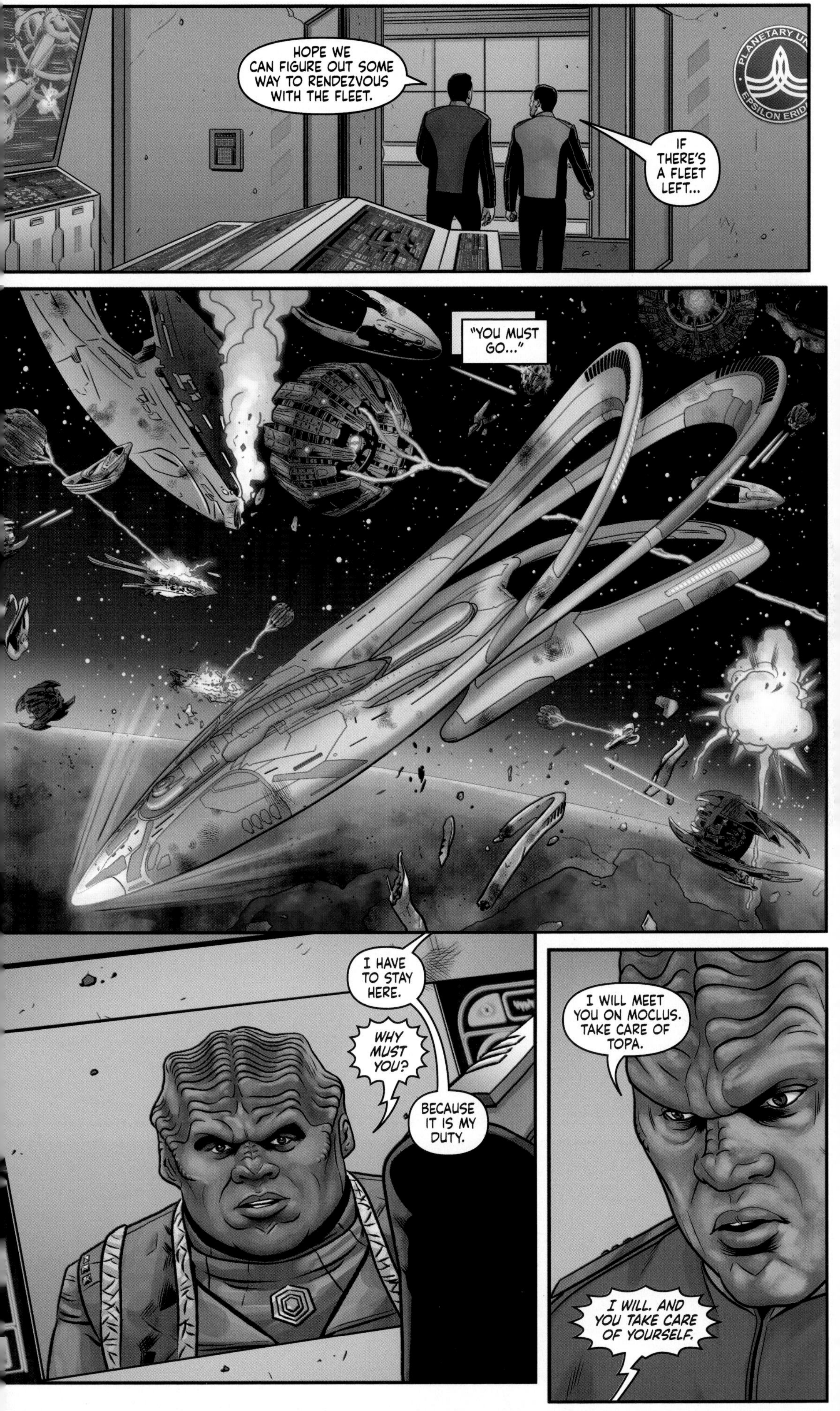
HOPE WE CAN FIGURE OUT SOME WAY TO RENDEZVOUS WITH THE FLEET.
IF THERE'S A FLEET LEFT...
PLANETARY UN
EPSILON ERID
"YOU MUST GO..."
I HAVE TO STAY HERE.
WHY MUST YOU?
BECAUSE IT IS MY DUTY.
I WILL MEET YOU ON MOCLUS. TAKE CARE OF TOPA.
I WILL. AND YOU TAKE CARE OF YOURSELF.

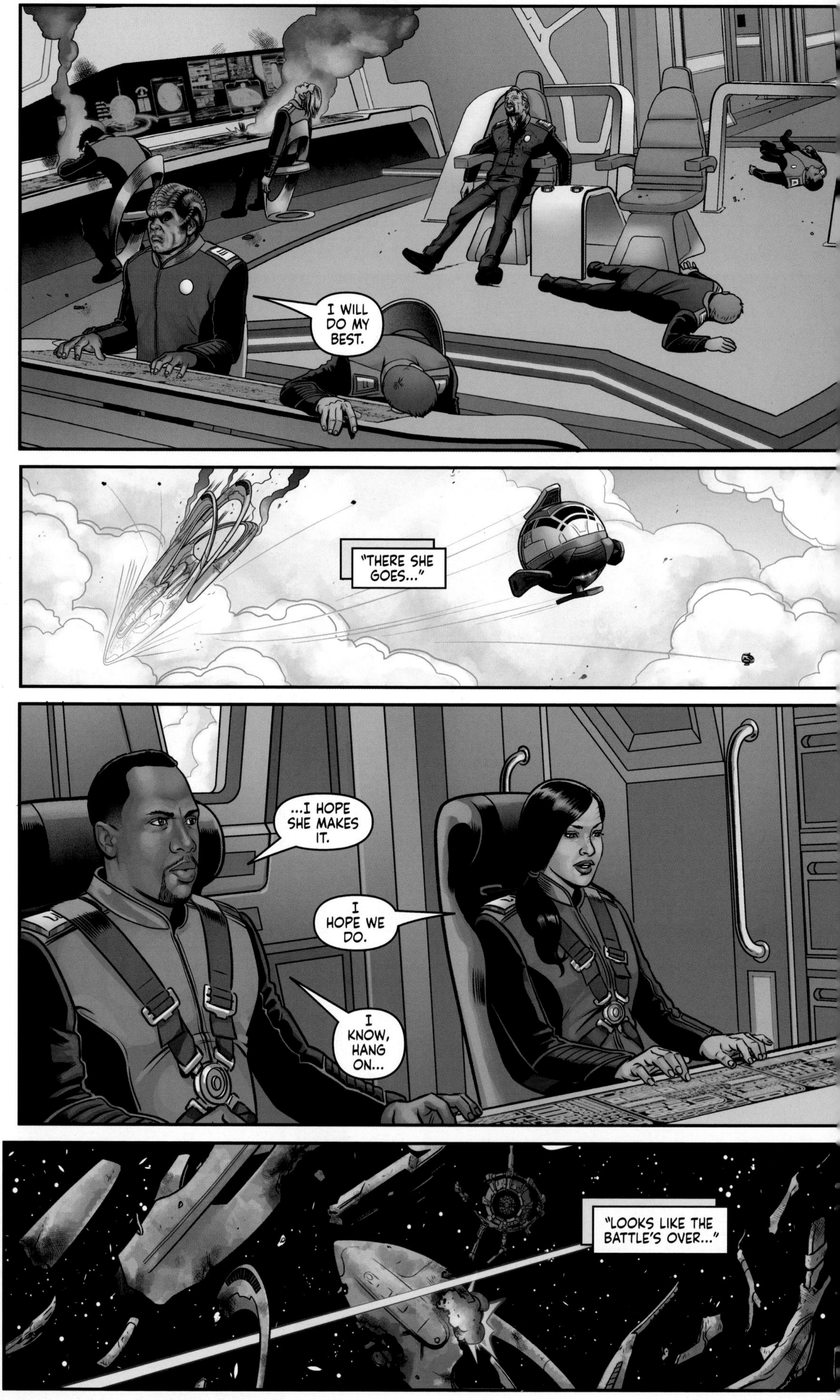
I WILL DO MY BEST.
"THERE SHE GOES..."
...I HOPE SHE MAKES IT.
I HOPE WE DO.
I KNOW, HANG ON...
"LOOKS LIKE THE BATTLE'S OVER..."

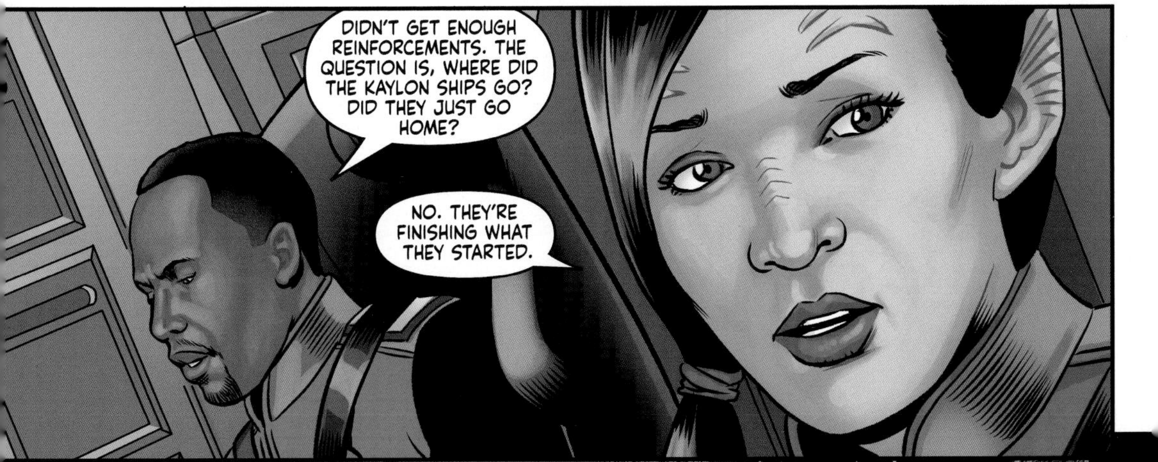
DIDN'T GET ENOUGH REINFORCEMENTS. THE QUESTION IS, WHERE DID THE KAYLON SHIPS GO? DID THEY JUST GO HOME?
NO. THEY'RE FINISHING WHAT THEY STARTED.

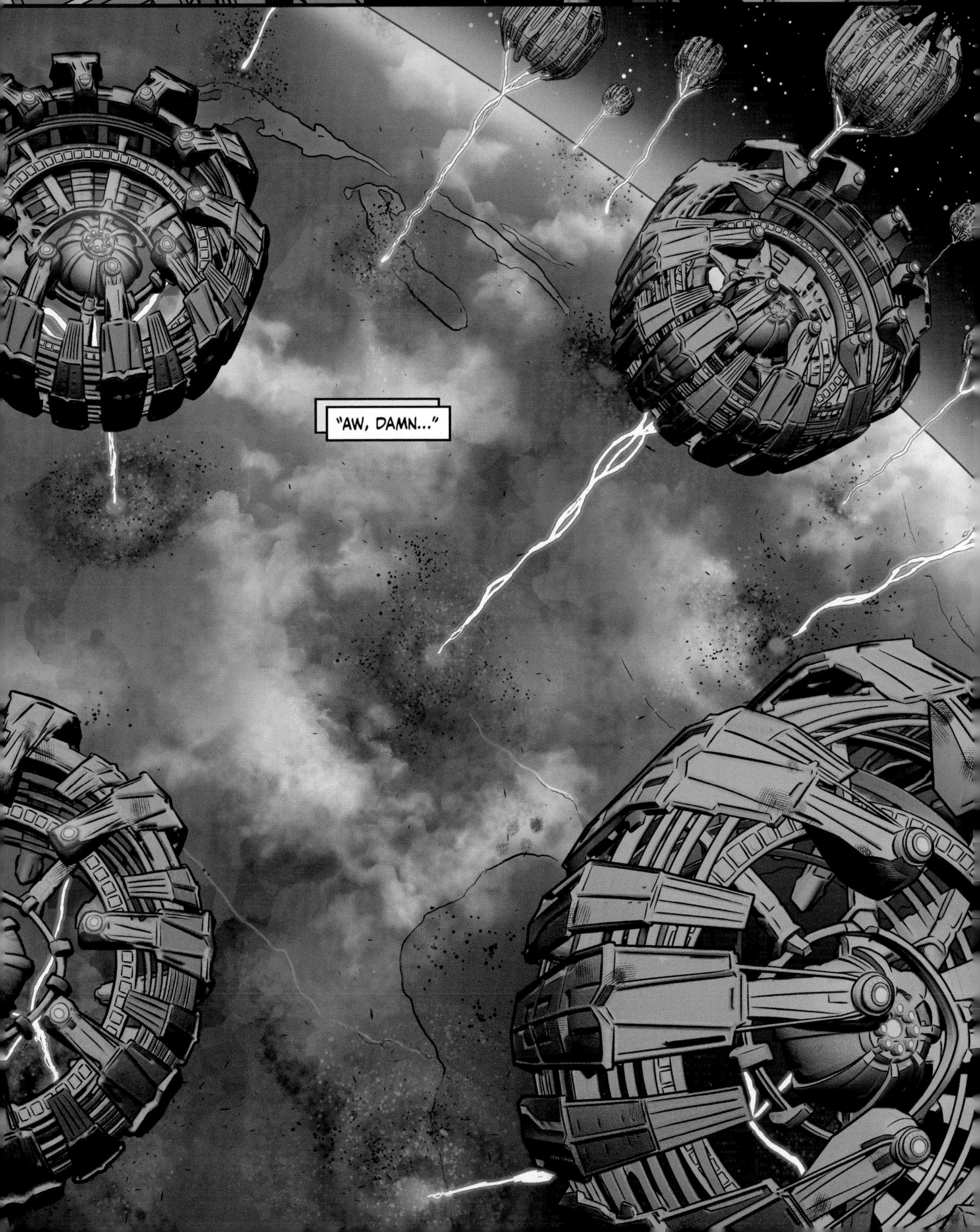
"AW, DAMN..."

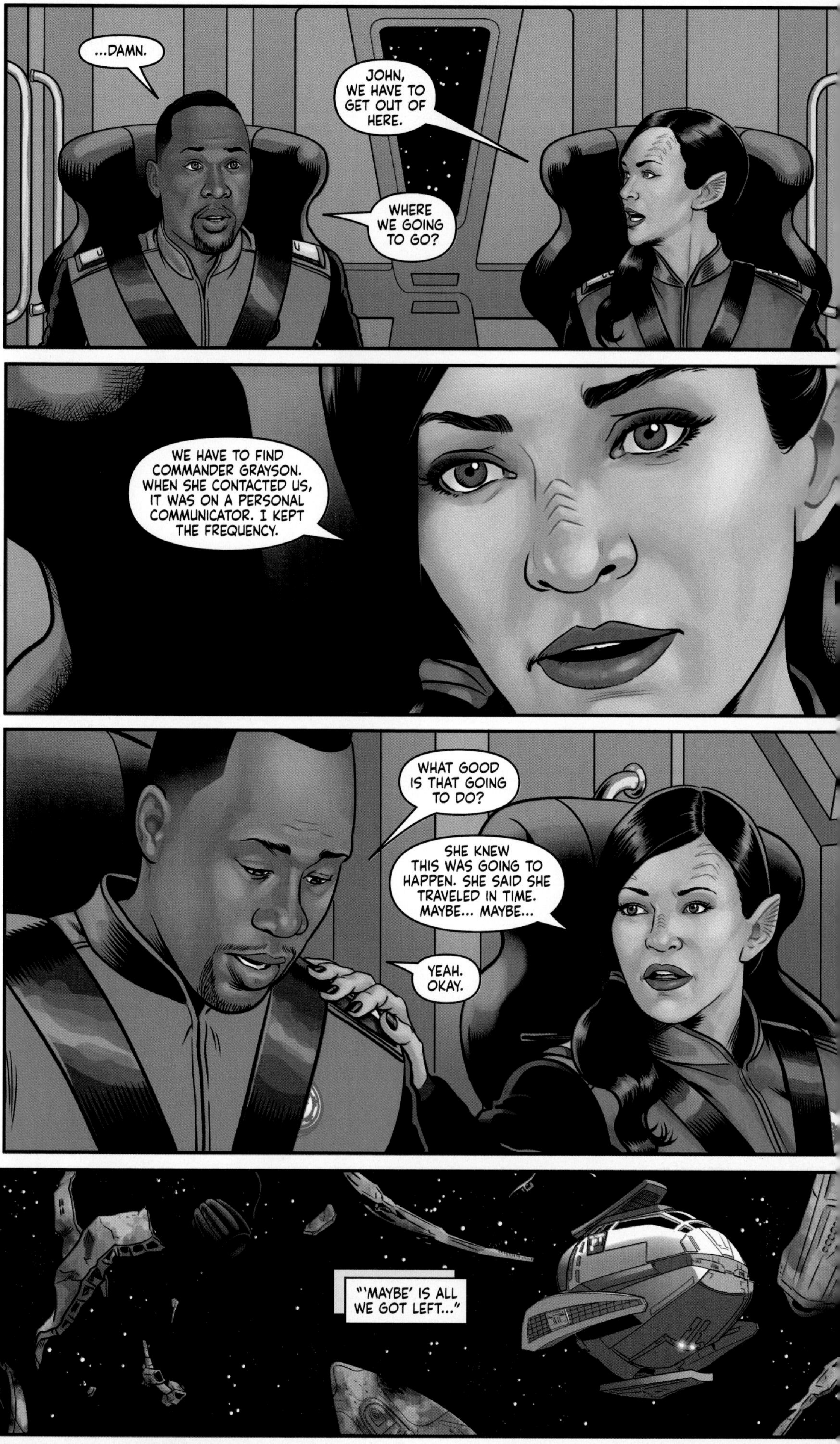
...DAMN.
JOHN, WE HAVE TO GET OUT OF HERE.
WHERE WE GOING TO GO?
WE HAVE TO FIND COMMANDER GRAYSON. WHEN SHE CONTACTED US, IT WAS ON A PERSONAL COMMUNICATOR. I KEPT THE FREQUENCY.
WHAT GOOD IS THAT GOING TO DO?
SHE KNEW THIS WAS GOING TO HAPPEN. SHE SAID SHE TRAVELED IN TIME. MAYBE... MAYBE...
YEAH. OKAY.
"'MAYBE' IS ALL WE GOT LEFT..."

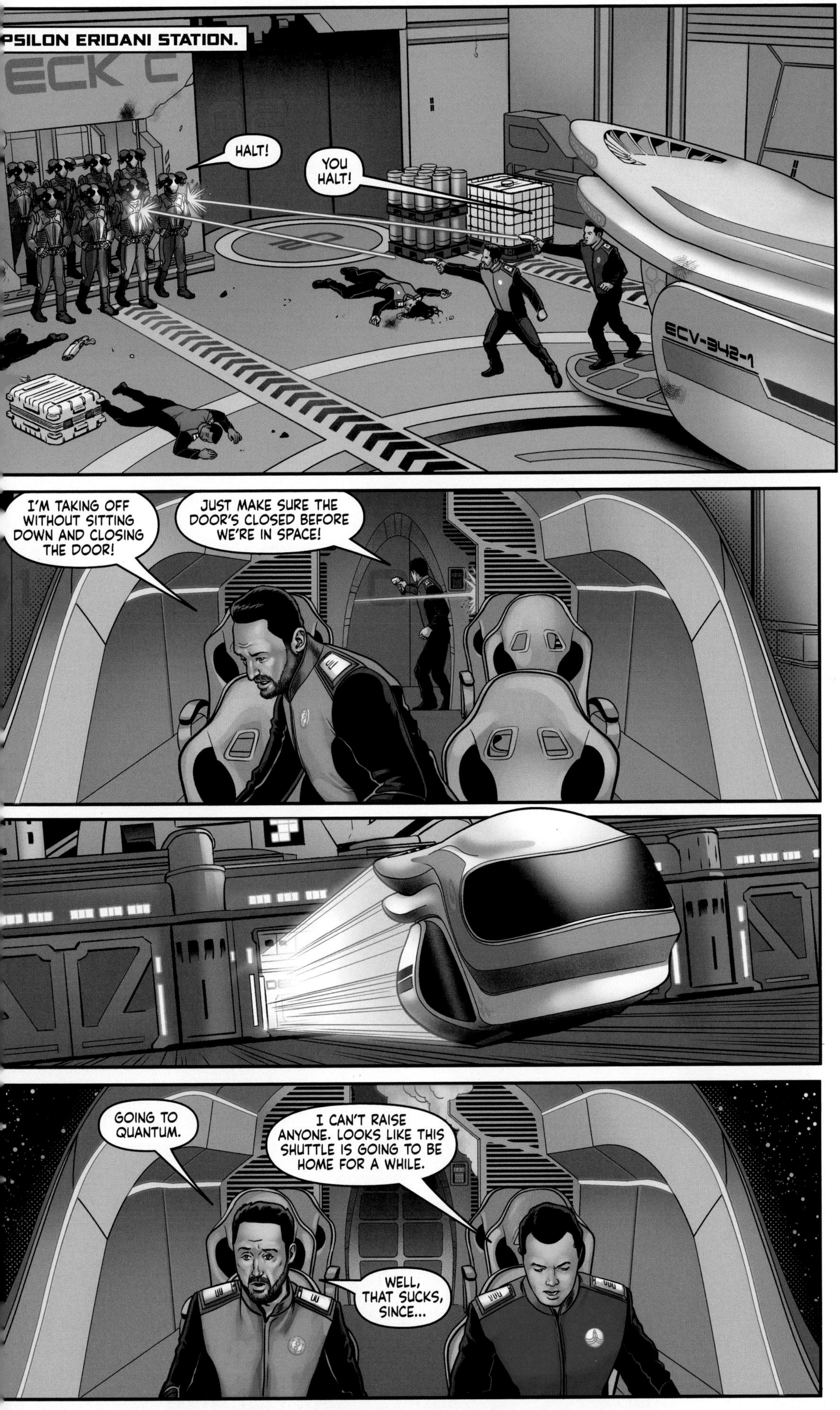
PSILON ERIDANI STATION.
ECK C
HALT!
YOU HALT!
ECV-342-1
I'M TAKING OFF WITHOUT SITTING DOWN AND CLOSING THE DOOR!
JUST MAKE SURE THE DOOR'S CLOSED BEFORE WE'RE IN SPACE!
GOING TO QUANTUM.
I CAN'T RAISE ANYONE. LOOKS LIKE THIS SHUTTLE IS GOING TO BE HOME FOR A WHILE.
WELL, THAT SUCKS, SINCE...

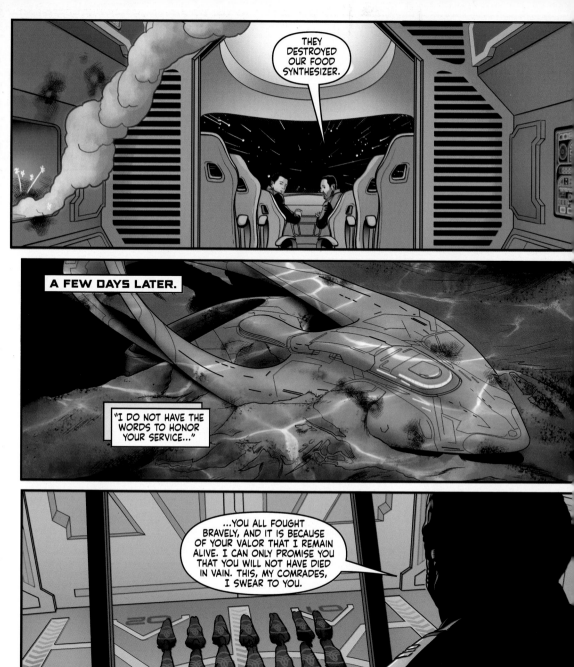

THEY DESTROYED OUR FOOD SYNTHESIZER.

A FEW DAYS LATER.

"I DO NOT HAVE THE WORDS TO HONOR YOUR SERVICE..."

...YOU ALL FOUGHT BRAVELY, AND IT IS BECAUSE OF YOUR VALOR THAT I REMAIN ALIVE. I CAN ONLY PROMISE YOU THAT YOU WILL NOT HAVE DIED IN VAIN. THIS, MY COMRADES, I SWEAR TO YOU.

I WILL REMEMBER YOU.

OPEN

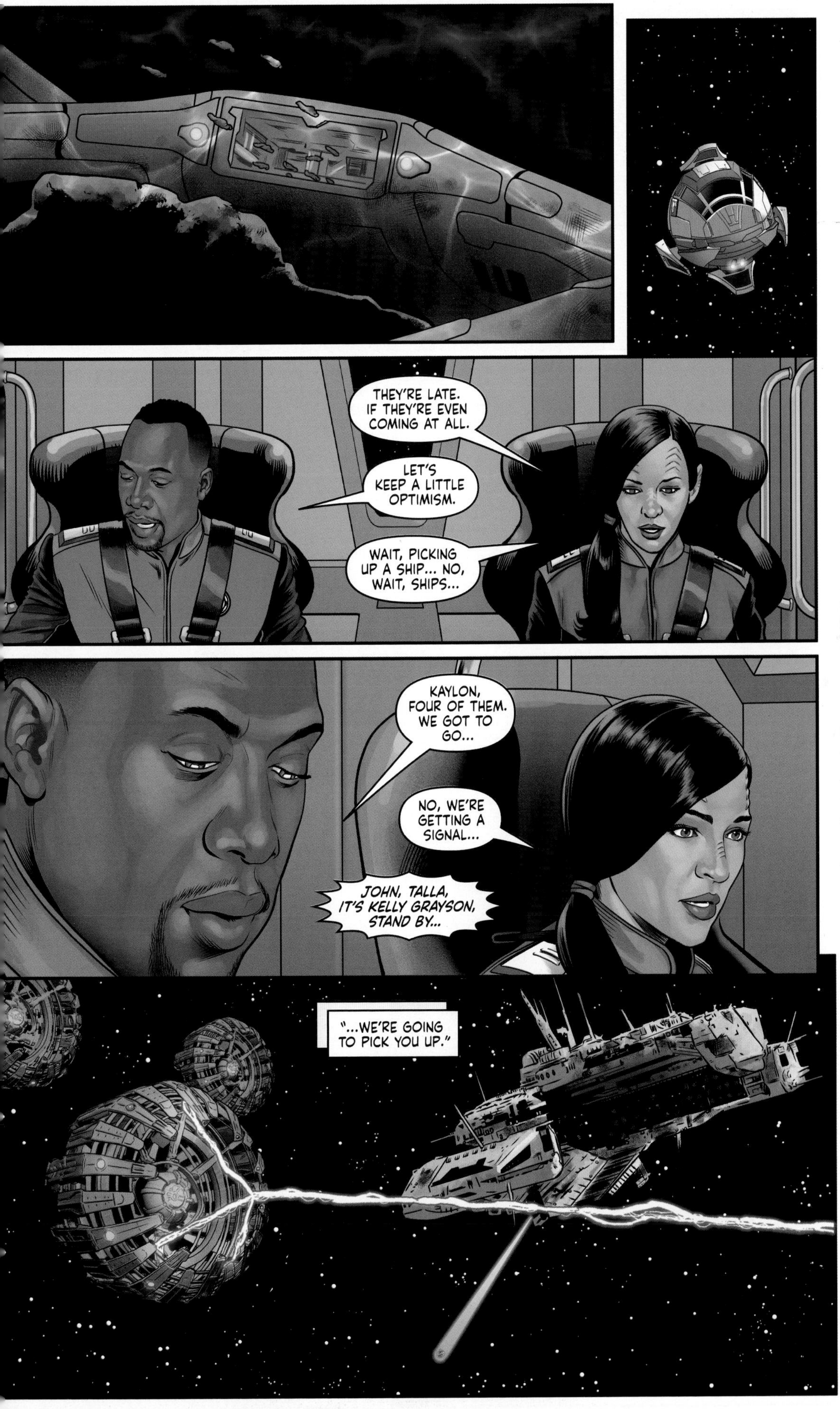
THEY'RE LATE. IF THEY'RE EVEN COMING AT ALL.
LET'S KEEP A LITTLE OPTIMISM.
WAIT, PICKING UP A SHIP... NO, WAIT, SHIPS...
KAYLON, FOUR OF THEM. WE GOT TO GO...
NO, WE'RE GETTING A SIGNAL...
JOHN, TALLA, IT'S KELLY GRAYSON, STAND BY...
"...WE'RE GOING TO PICK YOU UP."

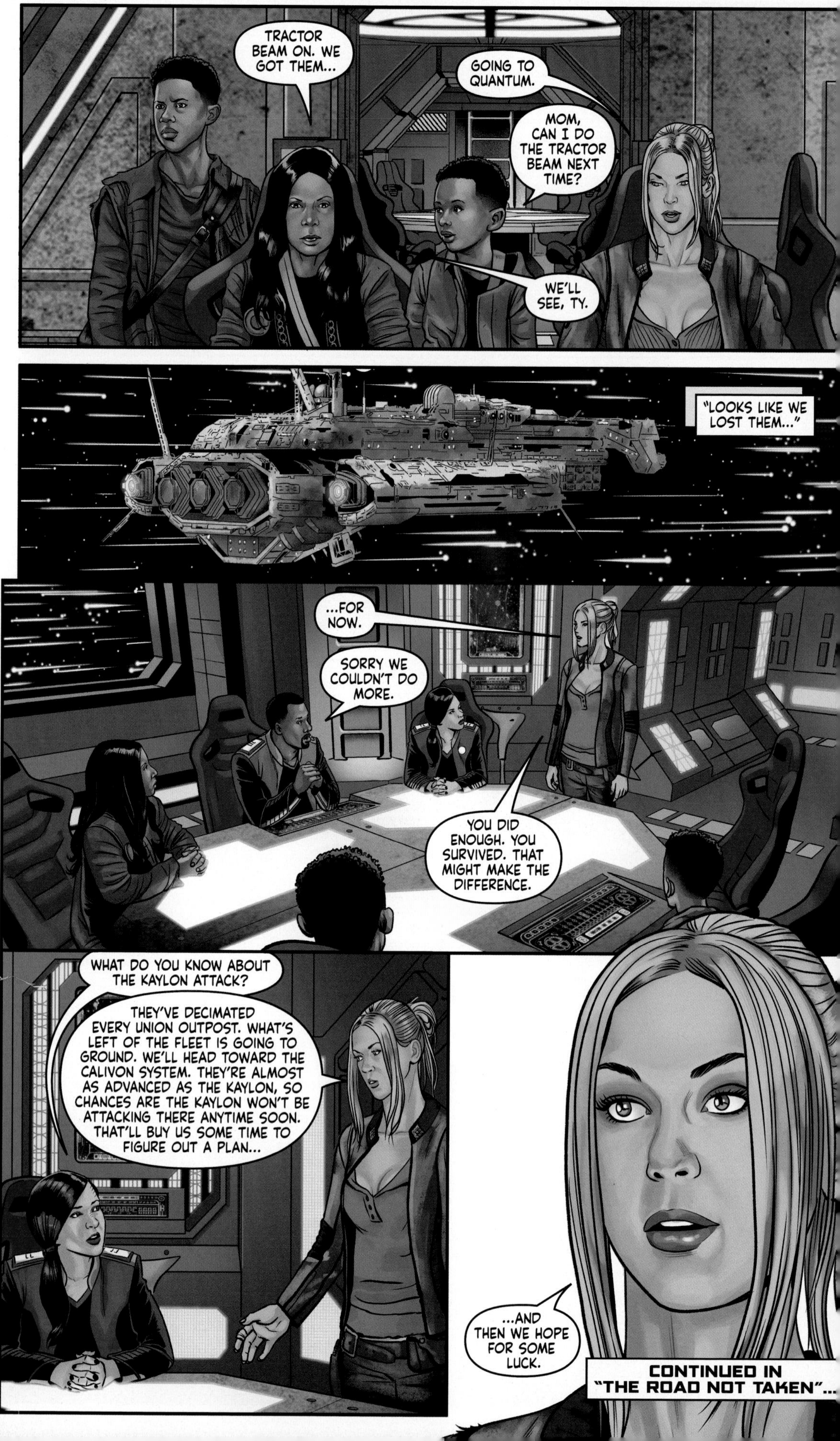

TRACTOR BEAM ON. WE GOT THEM...
GOING TO QUANTUM.
MOM, CAN I DO THE TRACTOR BEAM NEXT TIME?
WE'LL SEE, TY.
"LOOKS LIKE WE LOST THEM..."
...FOR NOW.
SORRY WE COULDN'T DO MORE.
YOU DID ENOUGH. YOU SURVIVED. THAT MIGHT MAKE THE DIFFERENCE.
WHAT DO YOU KNOW ABOUT THE KAYLON ATTACK?
THEY'VE DECIMATED EVERY UNION OUTPOST. WHAT'S LEFT OF THE FLEET IS GOING TO GROUND. WE'LL HEAD TOWARD THE CALIVON SYSTEM. THEY'RE ALMOST AS ADVANCED AS THE KAYLON, SO CHANCES ARE THE KAYLON WON'T BE ATTACKING THERE ANYTIME SOON. THAT'LL BUY US SOME TIME TO FIGURE OUT A PLAN...
...AND THEN WE HOPE FOR SOME LUCK.
CONTINUED IN "THE ROAD NOT TAKEN"...

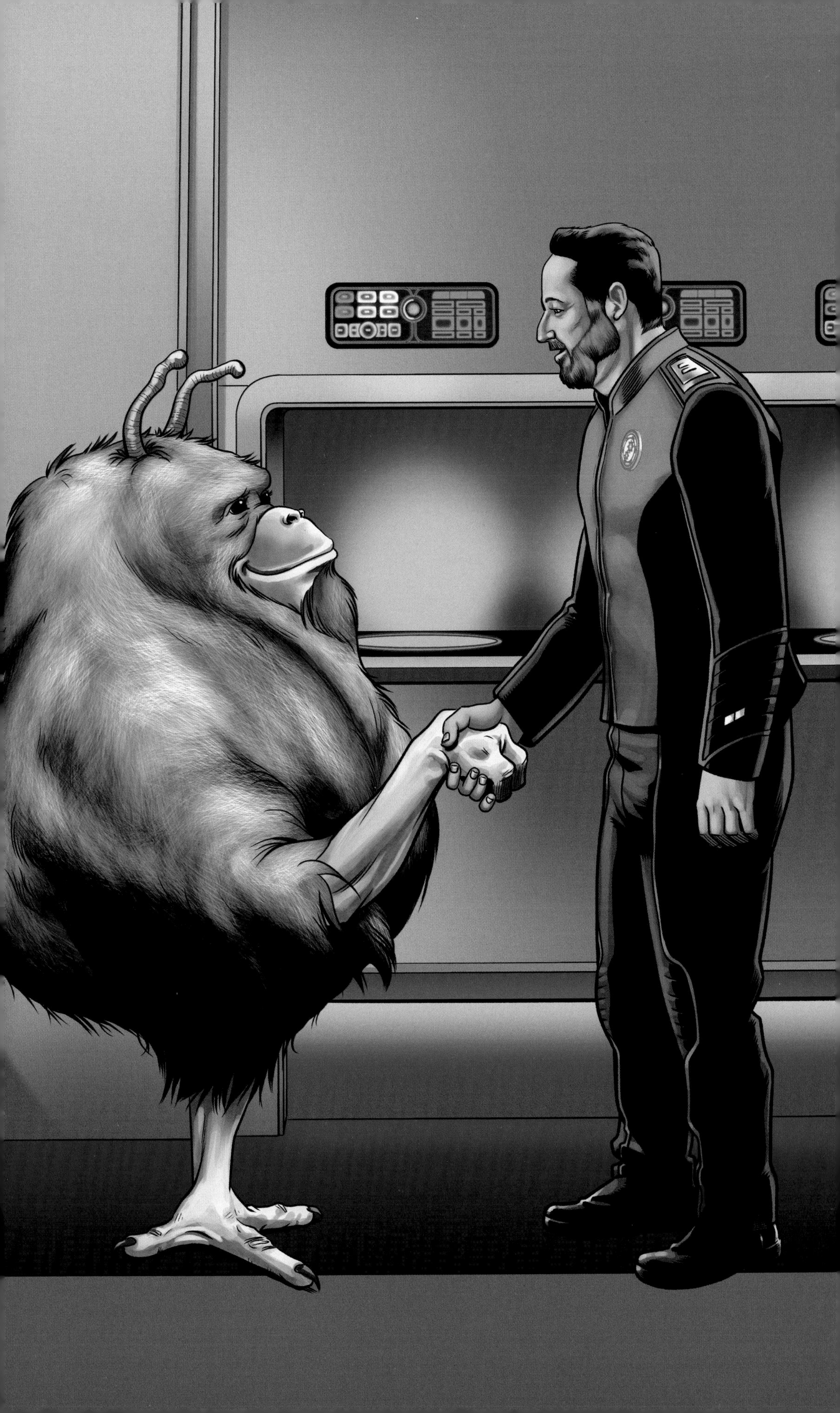

ARTIFACTS PART 1

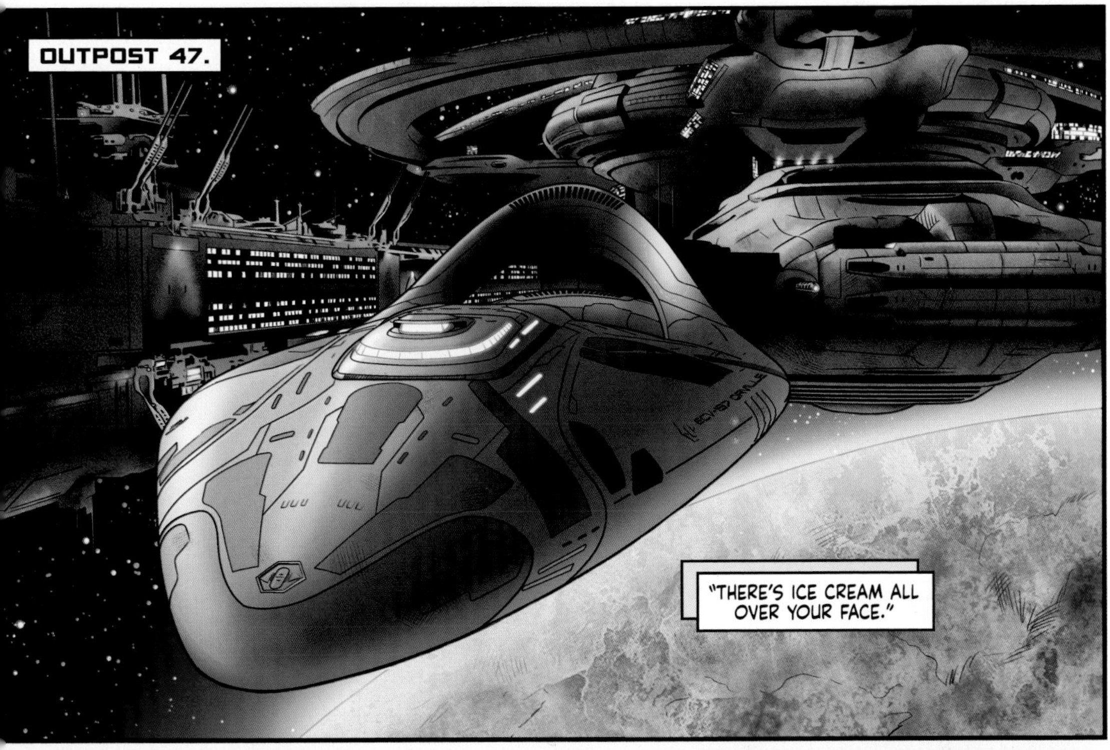
OUTPOST 47.
"THERE'S ICE CREAM ALL OVER YOUR FACE."

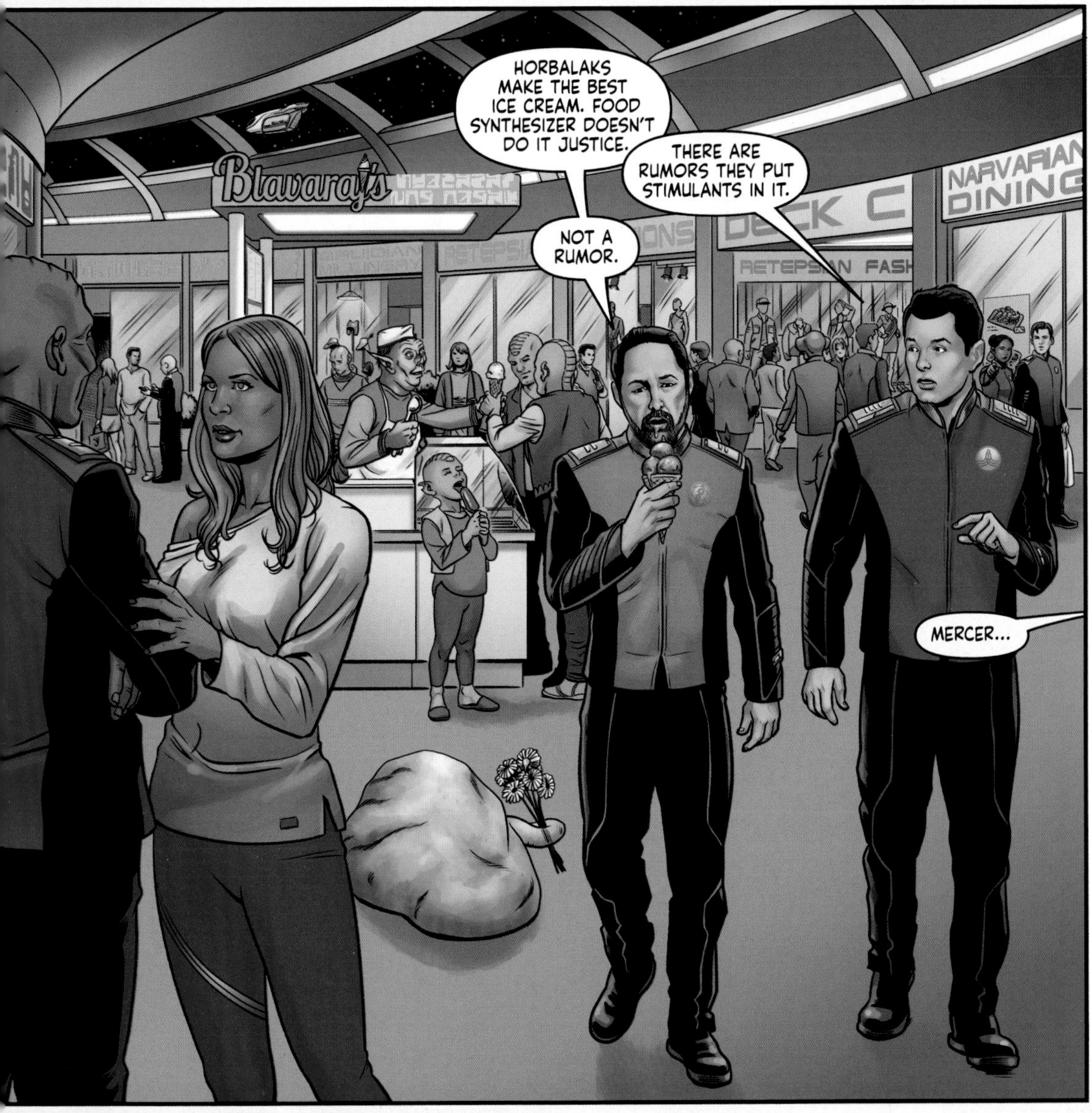
Blavaraj's
HORBALAKS MAKE THE BEST ICE CREAM. FOOD SYNTHESIZER DOESN'T DO IT JUSTICE.
THERE ARE RUMORS THEY PUT STIMULANTS IN IT.
NOT A RUMOR.
NARVARIAN DINING
RETEPSIAN FASH
MERCER...

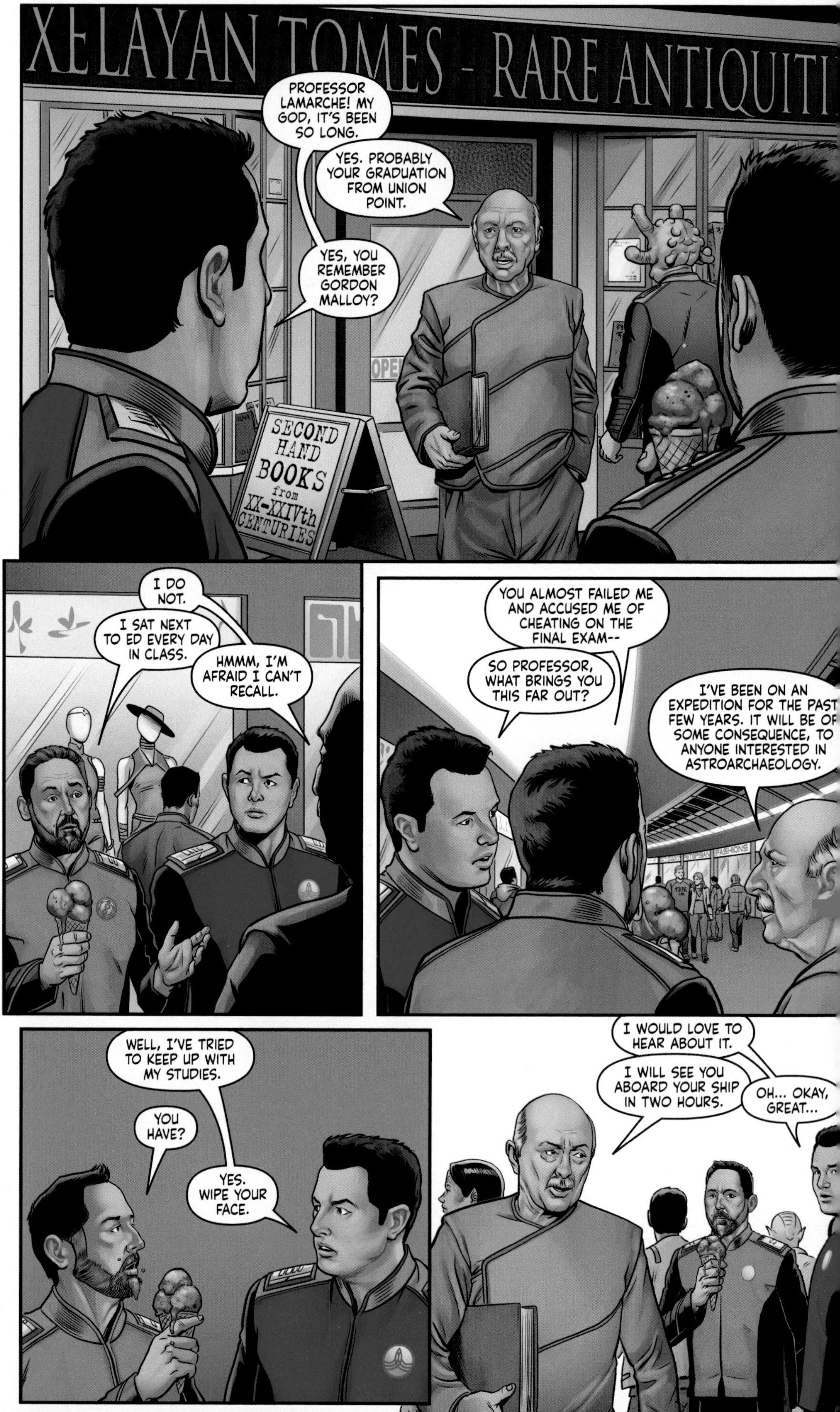
XELAYAN TOMES - RARE ANTIQUITI
PROFESSOR LAMARCHE! MY GOD, IT'S BEEN SO LONG.
YES. PROBABLY YOUR GRADUATION FROM UNION POINT.
YES, YOU REMEMBER GORDON MALLOY?
OPEN
SECOND HAND BOOKS from XX-XXIVth CENTURIES
I DO NOT.
I SAT NEXT TO ED EVERY DAY IN CLASS.
HMMM, I'M AFRAID I CAN'T RECALL.
YOU ALMOST FAILED ME AND ACCUSED ME OF CHEATING ON THE FINAL EXAM--
SO PROFESSOR, WHAT BRINGS YOU THIS FAR OUT?
I'VE BEEN ON AN EXPEDITION FOR THE PAST FEW YEARS. IT WILL BE OF SOME CONSEQUENCE, TO ANYONE INTERESTED IN ASTROARCHAEOLOGY.
FASHIONS
WELL, I'VE TRIED TO KEEP UP WITH MY STUDIES.
YOU HAVE?
YES. WIPE YOUR FACE.
I WOULD LOVE TO HEAR ABOUT IT.
I WILL SEE YOU ABOARD YOUR SHIP IN TWO HOURS.
OH... OKAY, GREAT...

I'LL BE THERE TOO. I'M THE HELMSMAN.

ASSHOLE REMEMBERED ME.

WIPE YOUR FACE.

"QUITE A SHIP YOU HAVE HERE..."

...YOU'VE DONE WELL FOR YOURSELF.

WELL, THERE'S ALWAYS SOMEONE DOING A LITTLE BETTER, BUT I CAN'T COMPLAIN. THE QUESTION IS WHAT HAVE YOU BEEN UP TO? YOUR PUBLISHED WORKS HAVE FALLEN OFF IN THE LAST COUPLE OF YEARS.

ALL CAREERS HAVE EBBS AND FLOWS. MINE IS EBBING. SO I DECIDED TO DEVOTE MYSELF TO THE ONE COURSE OF STUDY THAT HAD THE MOST POTENTIAL FOR ME TO LEAVE A MARK.

THE ZANKON?

EXACTLY. AND YOU CAN BE A PART OF IT.

REALLY? HOW?

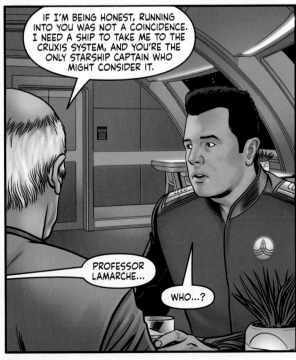

IF I'M BEING HONEST, RUNNING INTO YOU WAS NOT A COINCIDENCE. I NEED A SHIP TO TAKE ME TO THE CRUXIS SYSTEM, AND YOU'RE THE ONLY STARSHIP CAPTAIN WHO MIGHT CONSIDER IT.

PROFESSOR LAMARCHE...

WHO...?

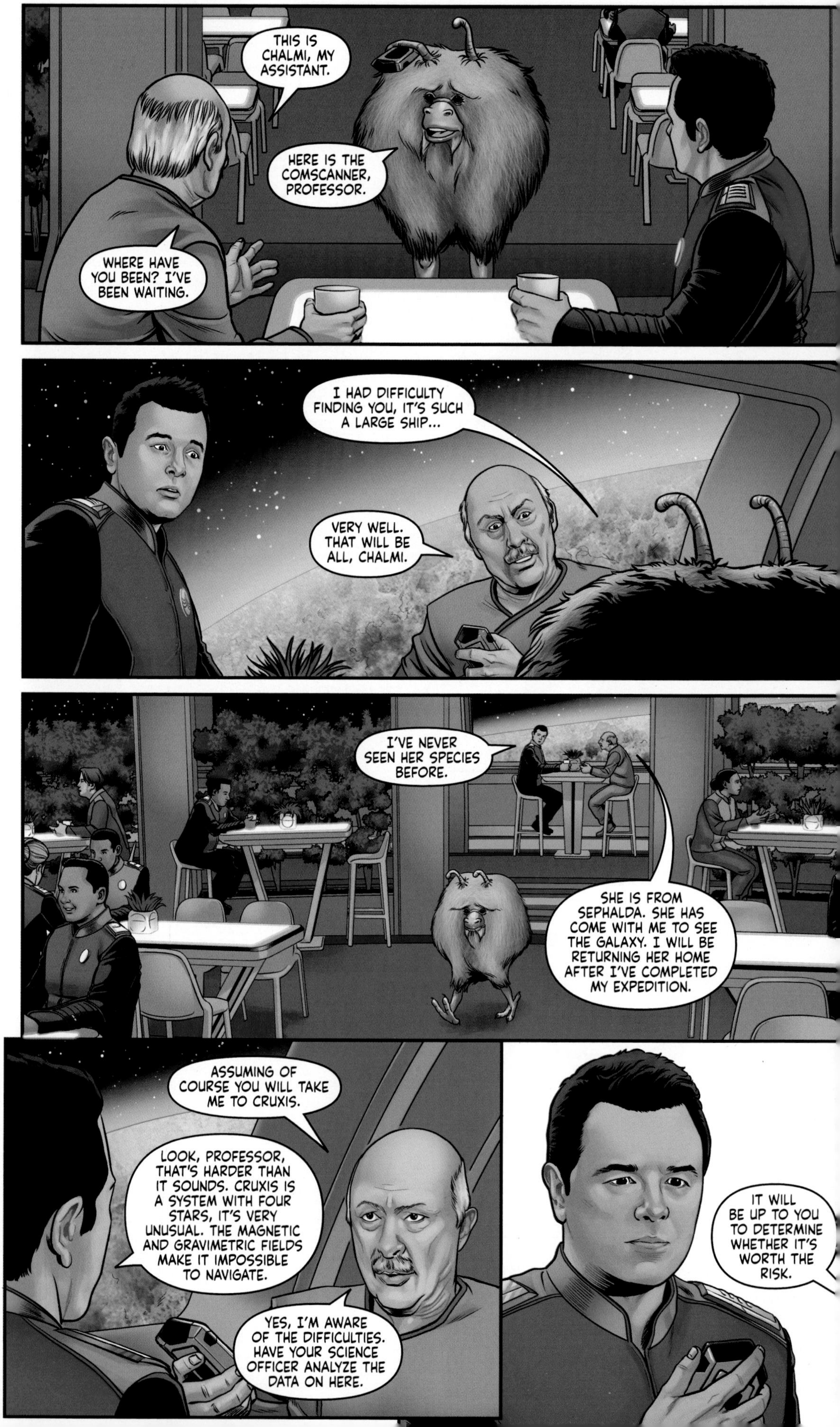
THIS IS CHALMI, MY ASSISTANT.
HERE IS THE COMSCANNER, PROFESSOR.
WHERE HAVE YOU BEEN? I'VE BEEN WAITING.
I HAD DIFFICULTY FINDING YOU, IT'S SUCH A LARGE SHIP...
VERY WELL. THAT WILL BE ALL, CHALMI.
I'VE NEVER SEEN HER SPECIES BEFORE.
SHE IS FROM SEPHALDA. SHE HAS COME WITH ME TO SEE THE GALAXY. I WILL BE RETURNING HER HOME AFTER I'VE COMPLETED MY EXPEDITION.
ASSUMING OF COURSE YOU WILL TAKE ME TO CRUXIS.
LOOK, PROFESSOR, THAT'S HARDER THAN IT SOUNDS. CRUXIS IS A SYSTEM WITH FOUR STARS, IT'S VERY UNUSUAL. THE MAGNETIC AND GRAVIMETRIC FIELDS MAKE IT IMPOSSIBLE TO NAVIGATE.
YES, I'M AWARE OF THE DIFFICULTIES. HAVE YOUR SCIENCE OFFICER ANALYZE THE DATA ON HERE.
IT WILL BE UP TO YOU TO DETERMINE WHETHER IT'S WORTH THE RISK.

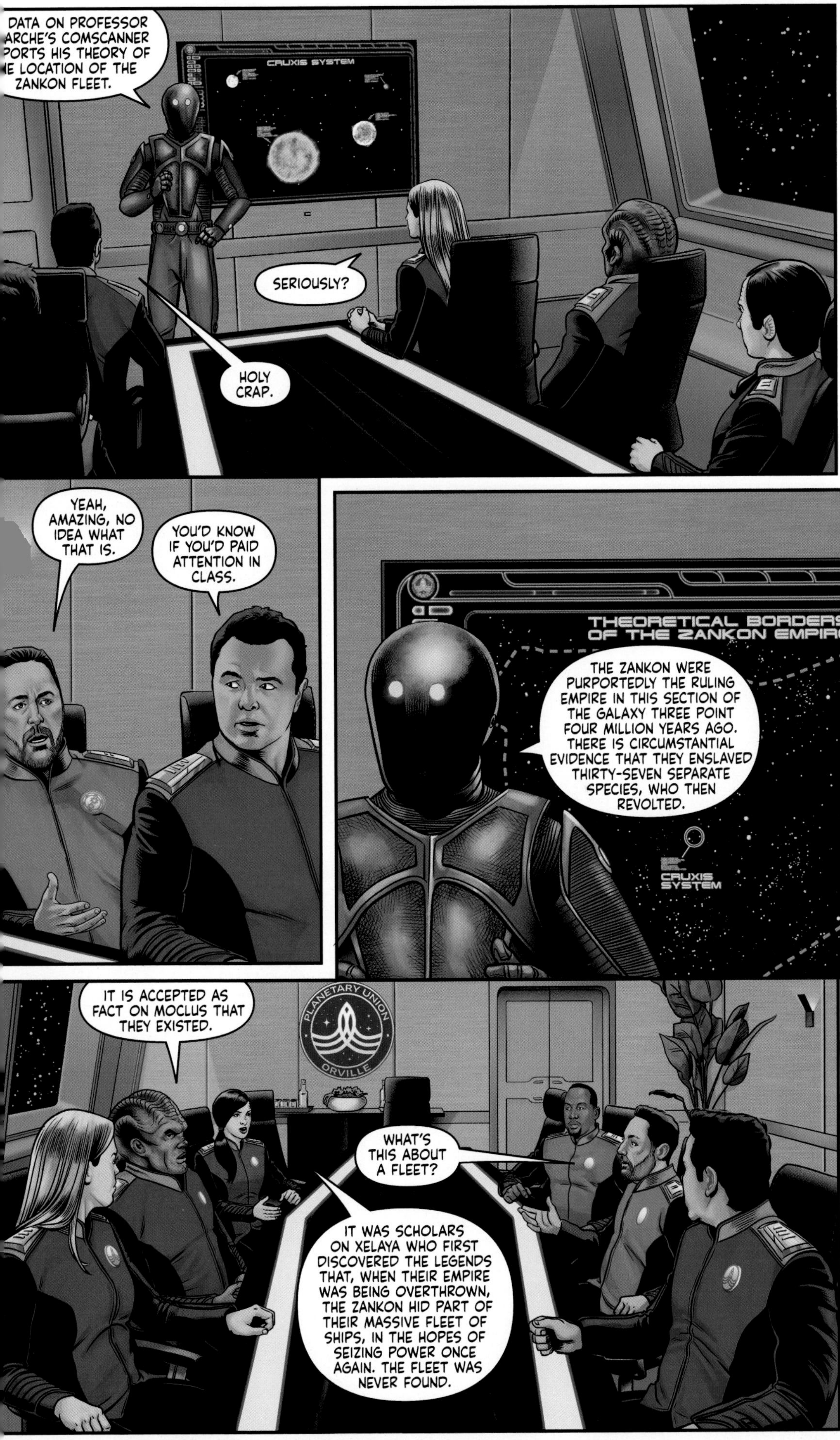
DATA ON PROFESSOR
ARCHE'S COMSCANNER
PORTS HIS THEORY OF
E LOCATION OF THE
ZANKON FLEET.
CRUXIS SYSTEM
SERIOUSLY?
HOLY CRAP.
YEAH, AMAZING, NO IDEA WHAT THAT IS.
YOU'D KNOW IF YOU'D PAID ATTENTION IN CLASS.
THEORETICAL BORDERS OF THE ZANKON EMPIRE
THE ZANKON WERE PURPORTEDLY THE RULING EMPIRE IN THIS SECTION OF THE GALAXY THREE POINT FOUR MILLION YEARS AGO. THERE IS CIRCUMSTANTIAL EVIDENCE THAT THEY ENSLAVED THIRTY-SEVEN SEPARATE SPECIES, WHO THEN REVOLTED.
CRUXIS SYSTEM
IT IS ACCEPTED AS FACT ON MOCLUS THAT THEY EXISTED.
PLANETARY UNION
ORVILLE
WHAT'S THIS ABOUT A FLEET?
IT WAS SCHOLARS ON XELAYA WHO FIRST DISCOVERED THE LEGENDS THAT, WHEN THEIR EMPIRE WAS BEING OVERTHROWN, THE ZANKON HID PART OF THEIR MASSIVE FLEET OF SHIPS, IN THE HOPES OF SEIZING POWER ONCE AGAIN. THE FLEET WAS NEVER FOUND.

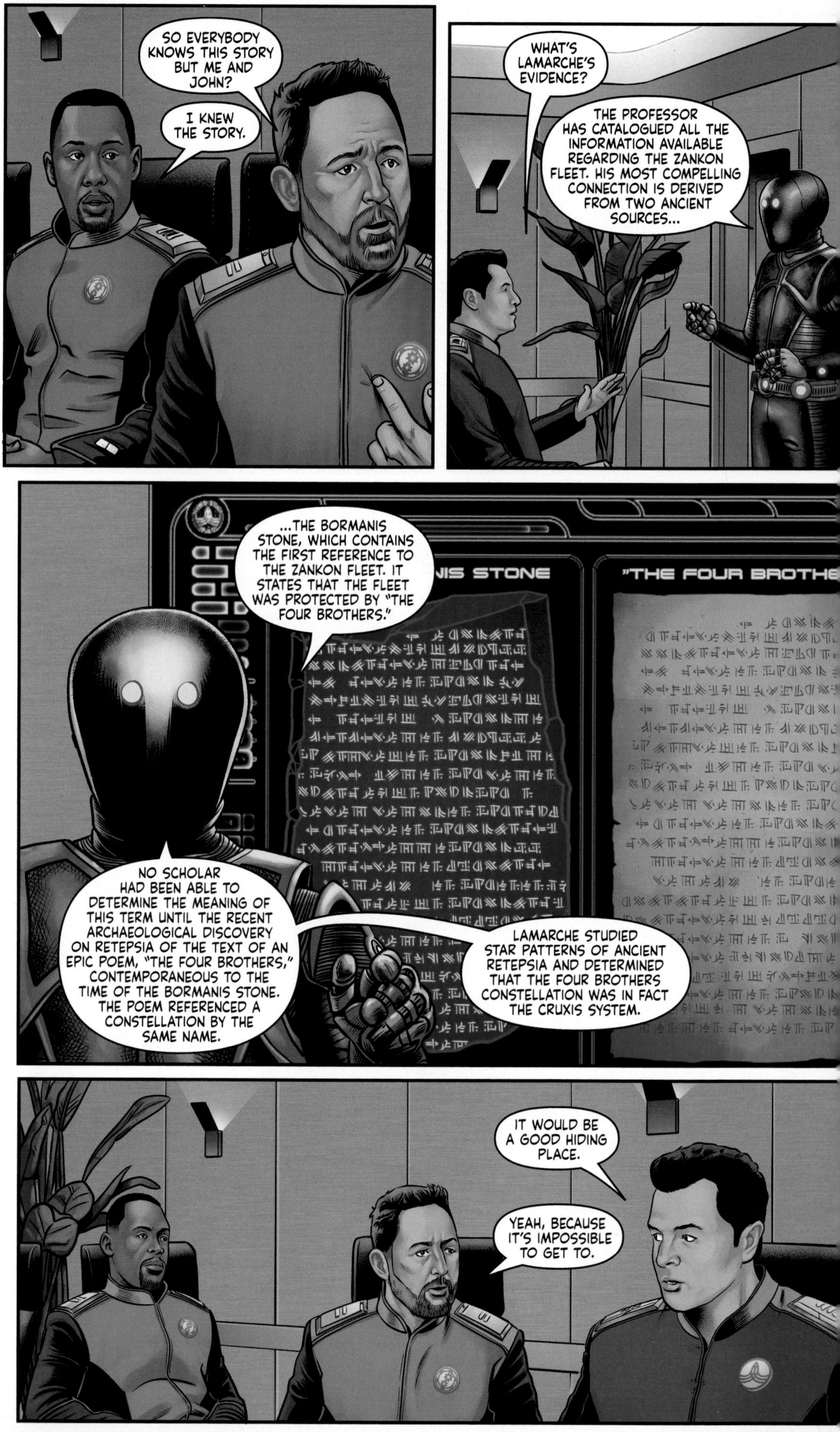
SO EVERYBODY KNOWS THIS STORY BUT ME AND JOHN?
I KNEW THE STORY.
WHAT'S LAMARCHE'S EVIDENCE?
THE PROFESSOR HAS CATALOGUED ALL THE INFORMATION AVAILABLE REGARDING THE ZANKON FLEET. HIS MOST COMPELLING CONNECTION IS DERIVED FROM TWO ANCIENT SOURCES...
...THE BORMANIS STONE, WHICH CONTAINS THE FIRST REFERENCE TO THE ZANKON FLEET. IT STATES THAT THE FLEET WAS PROTECTED BY "THE FOUR BROTHERS."
NIS STONE
"THE FOUR BROTHE
NO SCHOLAR HAD BEEN ABLE TO DETERMINE THE MEANING OF THIS TERM UNTIL THE RECENT ARCHAEOLOGICAL DISCOVERY ON RETEPSIA OF THE TEXT OF AN EPIC POEM, "THE FOUR BROTHERS," CONTEMPORANEOUS TO THE TIME OF THE BORMANIS STONE. THE POEM REFERENCED A CONSTELLATION BY THE SAME NAME.
LAMARCHE STUDIED STAR PATTERNS OF ANCIENT RETEPSIA AND DETERMINED THAT THE FOUR BROTHERS CONSTELLATION WAS IN FACT THE CRUXIS SYSTEM.
IT WOULD BE A GOOD HIDING PLACE.
YEAH, BECAUSE IT'S IMPOSSIBLE TO GET TO.

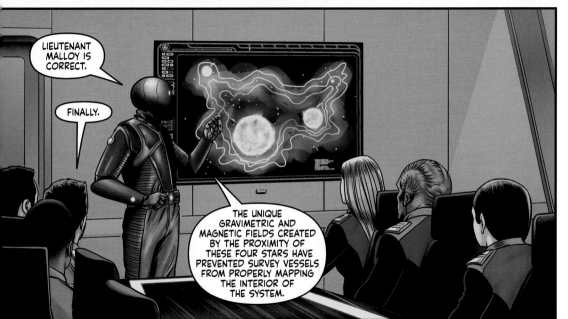

LIEUTENANT MALLOY IS CORRECT.

FINALLY.

THE UNIQUE GRAVIMETRIC AND MAGNETIC FIELDS CREATED BY THE PROXIMITY OF THESE FOUR STARS HAVE PREVENTED SURVEY VESSELS FROM PROPERLY MAPPING THE INTERIOR OF THE SYSTEM.

WHICH MEANS... THOSE SHIPS COULD STILL BE THERE. EVEN AFTER THREE MILLION YEARS.

ONLY ONE WAY TO FIND OUT.

I'M NOT SURE FOLLOWING PROFESSOR LAMARCHE IS ADVISABLE.

WHY NOT?

LAMARCHE WAS REMOVED FROM HIS POSITION AT UNION POINT BECAUSE OF SOME OVERZEALOUSNESS REGARDING HIS ZANKON THEORIES. HE'S BEEN SHUNNED BY THE UNION SCIENTIFIC COMMUNITY.

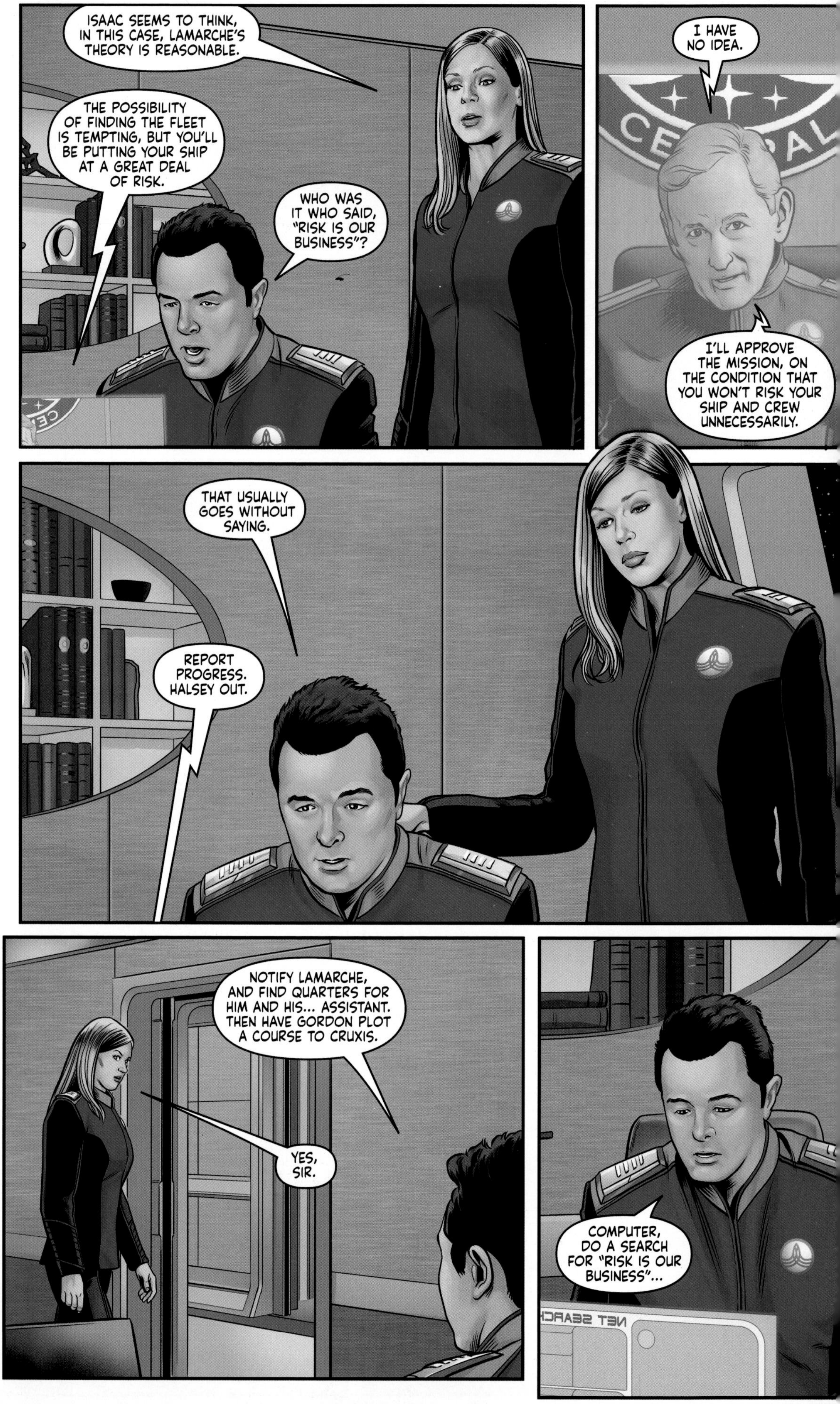
ISAAC SEEMS TO THINK, IN THIS CASE, LAMARCHE'S THEORY IS REASONABLE.
THE POSSIBILITY OF FINDING THE FLEET IS TEMPTING, BUT YOU'LL BE PUTTING YOUR SHIP AT A GREAT DEAL OF RISK.
WHO WAS IT WHO SAID, "RISK IS OUR BUSINESS"?
I HAVE NO IDEA.
I'LL APPROVE THE MISSION, ON THE CONDITION THAT YOU WON'T RISK YOUR SHIP AND CREW UNNECESSARILY.
THAT USUALLY GOES WITHOUT SAYING.
REPORT PROGRESS. HALSEY OUT.
NOTIFY LAMARCHE, AND FIND QUARTERS FOR HIM AND HIS... ASSISTANT. THEN HAVE GORDON PLOT A COURSE TO CRUXIS.
YES, SIR.
COMPUTER, DO A SEARCH FOR "RISK IS OUR BUSINESS"...
NET SEARCH

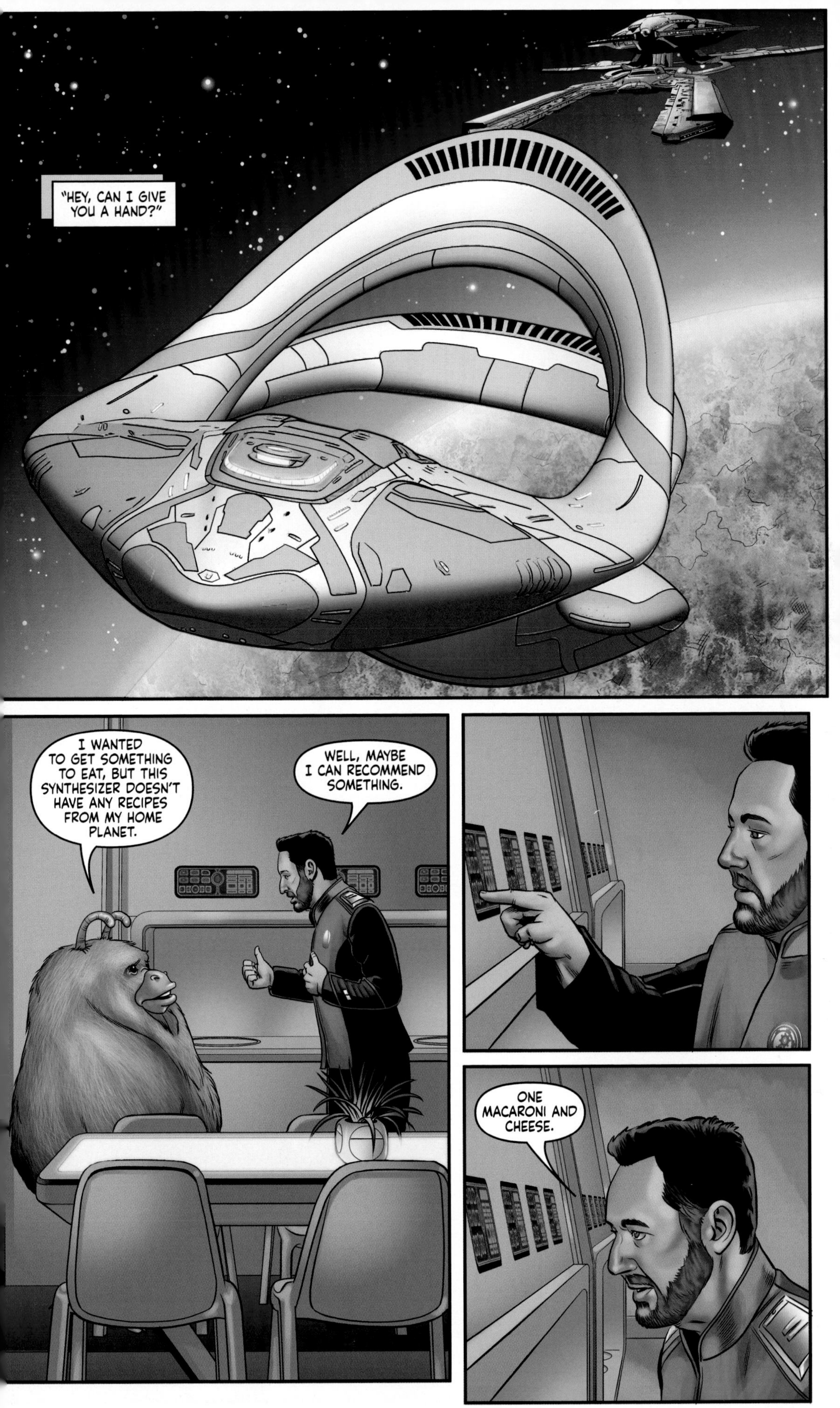
"HEY, CAN I GIVE YOU A HAND?"
I WANTED TO GET SOMETHING TO EAT, BUT THIS SYNTHESIZER DOESN'T HAVE ANY RECIPES FROM MY HOME PLANET.
WELL, MAYBE I CAN RECOMMEND SOMETHING.
ONE MACARONI AND CHEESE.

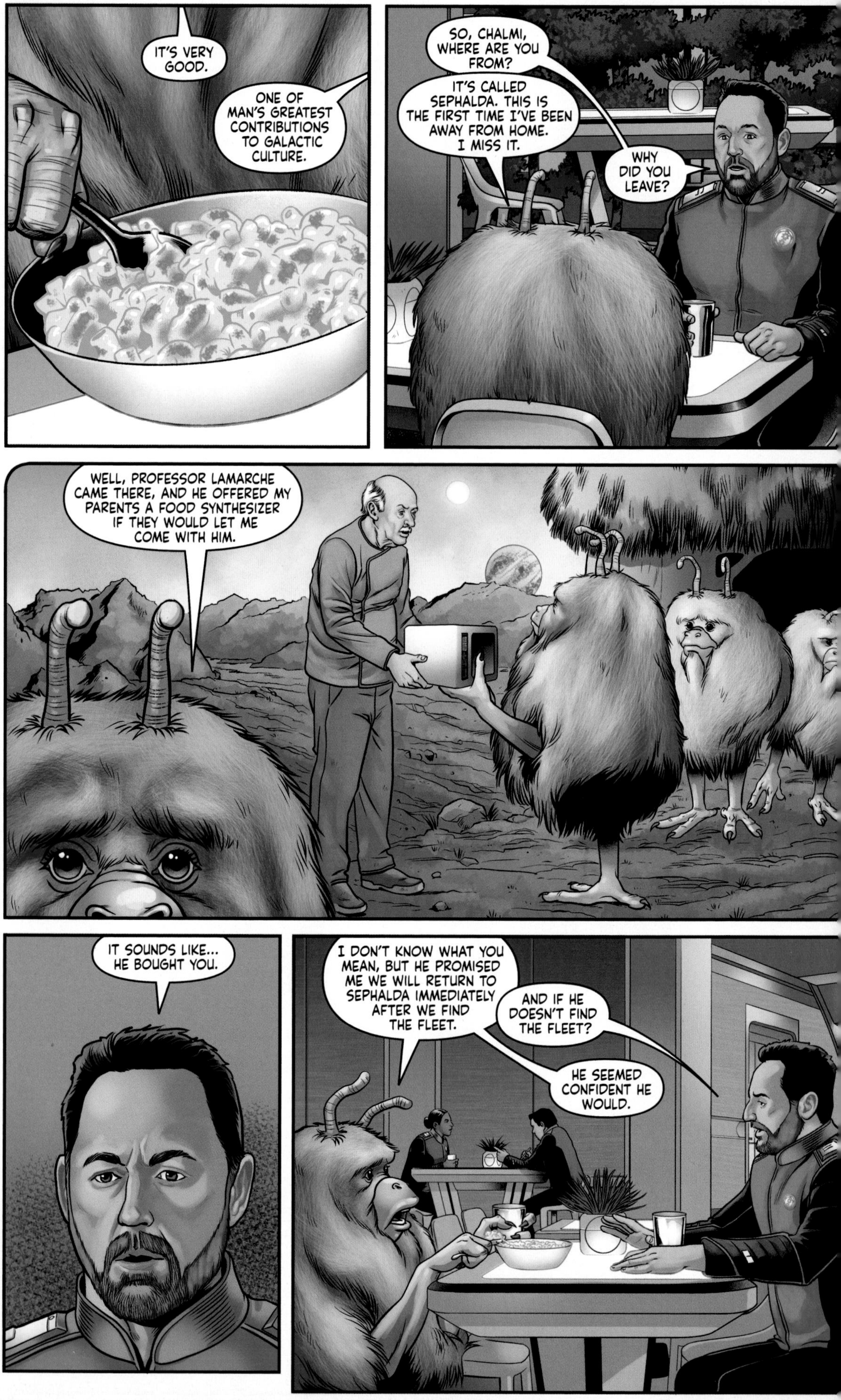
IT'S VERY GOOD.
ONE OF MAN'S GREATEST CONTRIBUTIONS TO GALACTIC CULTURE.
SO, CHALMI, WHERE ARE YOU FROM?
IT'S CALLED SEPHALDA. THIS IS THE FIRST TIME I'VE BEEN AWAY FROM HOME. I MISS IT.
WHY DID YOU LEAVE?
WELL, PROFESSOR LAMARCHE CAME THERE, AND HE OFFERED MY PARENTS A FOOD SYNTHESIZER IF THEY WOULD LET ME COME WITH HIM.
IT SOUNDS LIKE... HE BOUGHT YOU.
I DON'T KNOW WHAT YOU MEAN, BUT HE PROMISED ME WE WILL RETURN TO SEPHALDA IMMEDIATELY AFTER WE FIND THE FLEET.
AND IF HE DOESN'T FIND THE FLEET?
HE SEEMED CONFIDENT HE WOULD.

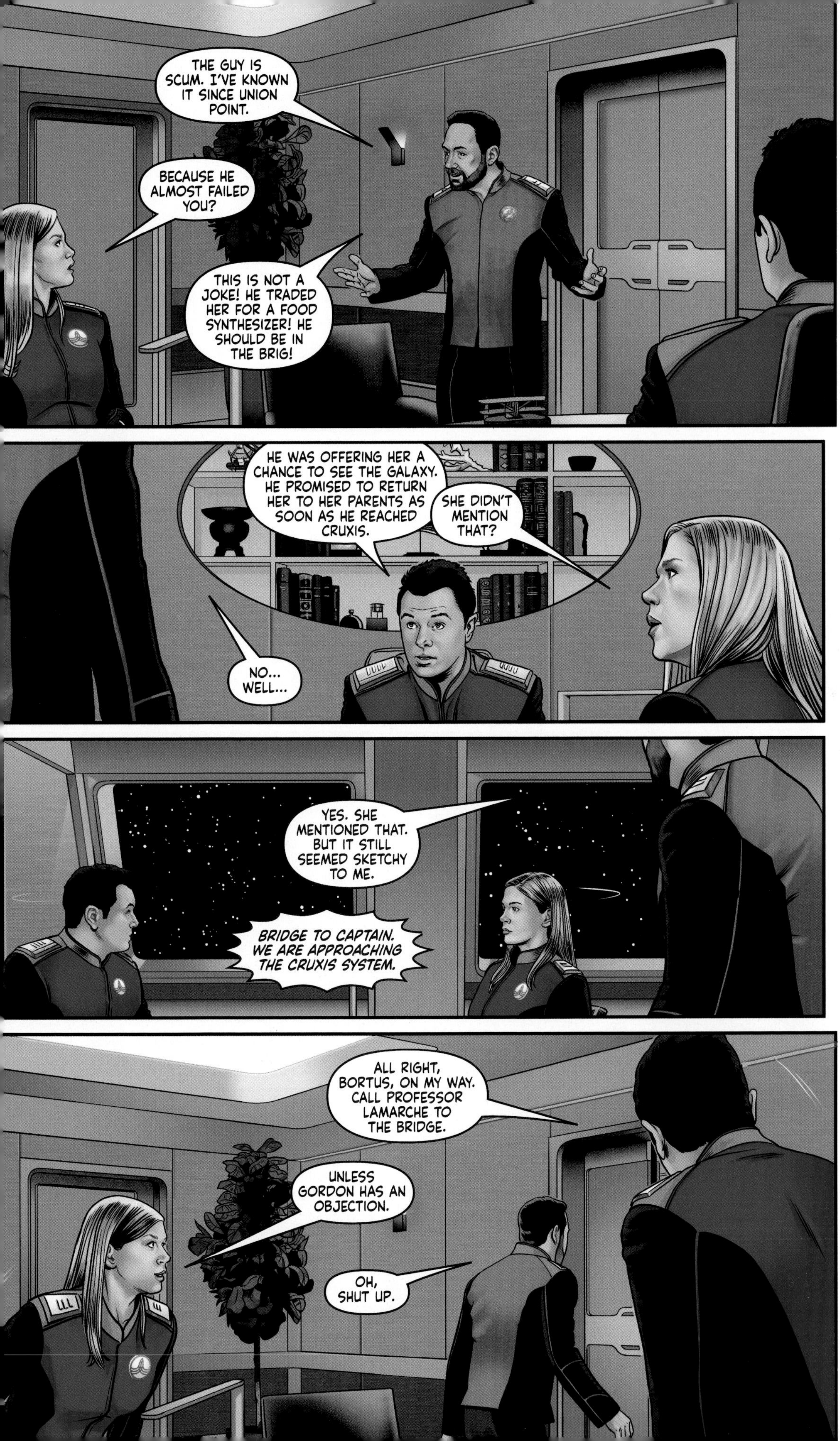
THE GUY IS SCUM. I'VE KNOWN IT SINCE UNION POINT.
BECAUSE HE ALMOST FAILED YOU?
THIS IS NOT A JOKE! HE TRADED HER FOR A FOOD SYNTHESIZER! HE SHOULD BE IN THE BRIG!
HE WAS OFFERING HER A CHANCE TO SEE THE GALAXY. HE PROMISED TO RETURN HER TO HER PARENTS AS SOON AS HE REACHED CRUXIS.
SHE DIDN'T MENTION THAT?
NO... WELL...
YES. SHE MENTIONED THAT. BUT IT STILL SEEMED SKETCHY TO ME.
BRIDGE TO CAPTAIN. WE ARE APPROACHING THE CRUXIS SYSTEM.
ALL RIGHT, BORTUS, ON MY WAY. CALL PROFESSOR LAMARCHE TO THE BRIDGE.
UNLESS GORDON HAS AN OBJECTION.
OH, SHUT UP.

"WE ARE THREE POINT SEVEN AU'S FROM THE OUTER PERIMETER..."

...OUR SENSORS CANNOT PENETRATE TO THE INTERIOR OF THE SYSTEM.

IT'S BEAUTIFUL.

AND DEADLY.

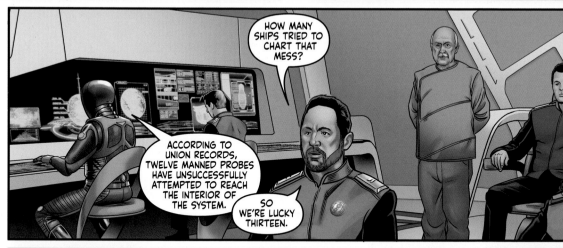

HOW MANY SHIPS TRIED TO CHART THAT MESS?

ACCORDING TO UNION RECORDS, TWELVE MANNED PROBES HAVE UNSUCCESSFULLY ATTEMPTED TO REACH THE INTERIOR OF THE SYSTEM.

SO WE'RE LUCKY THIRTEEN.

CAPTAIN, WE CAN STAY HERE AND CONTEMPLATE ANCIENT SUPERSTITIONS REGARDING NUMBERS OR WE CAN MAKE HISTORY.

YOU'RE RIGHT. WE'LL GIVE IT A SHOT.

HELM, TAKE US IN.

"CAPTAIN, READING AN INCREASE IN SOLAR ACTIVITY..."

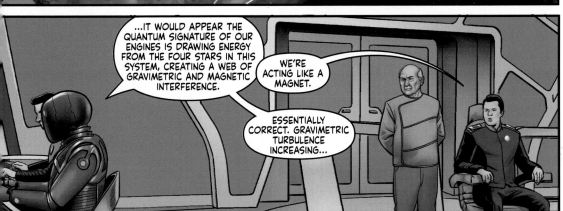

...IT WOULD APPEAR THE QUANTUM SIGNATURE OF OUR ENGINES IS DRAWING ENERGY FROM THE FOUR STARS IN THIS SYSTEM, CREATING A WEB OF GRAVIMETRIC AND MAGNETIC INTERFERENCE.

WE'RE ACTING LIKE A MAGNET.

ESSENTIALLY CORRECT. GRAVIMETRIC TURBULENCE INCREASING...

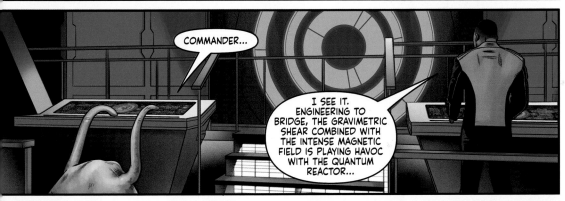

COMMANDER...

I SEE IT. ENGINEERING TO BRIDGE, THE GRAVIMETRIC SHEAR COMBINED WITH THE INTENSE MAGNETIC FIELD IS PLAYING HAVOC WITH THE QUANTUM REACTOR...

...WE KEEP THIS UP, WE COULD HAVE A CATASTROPHIC FAILURE.

UNDERSTOOD. ISAAC, HOW LONG TILL WE'RE THROUGH THIS TURBULENCE?

I AM UNABLE TO MAKE THAT DETERMINATION. SENSORS WILL NOT PENETRATE BEHIND THE PERIMETER.

WE HAVE A HULL BREACH ON DECK C.

DAMAGE CONTROL TEAM...

ENGINEERING TO BRIDGE, WE HAVE A NEW PROBLEM...

STRUCTURAL INTEGRITY ON THE UPPER RING IS DEGRADING...

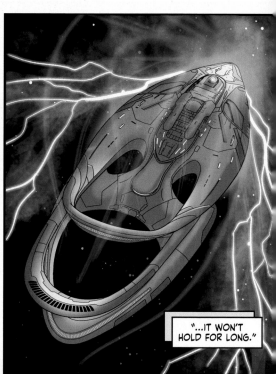

"...IT WON'T HOLD FOR LONG."

CAPTAIN, FORWARD MOMENTUM HAS STOPPED. WE'RE NOT MOVING...

CAN WE INCREASE POWER?

PROBABLY WANT TO CHECK WITH JOHN, BUT I THINK YOU KNOW WHAT HE'S GOING TO SAY...

I THINK I REMEMBER THE ADMIRAL SAYING SOMETHING ABOUT NOT PUTTING THE SHIP IN UNNECESSARY DANGER.

I REMEMBER THAT TOO. GORDON, BACK US OFF...

NO! YOU CAN'T!

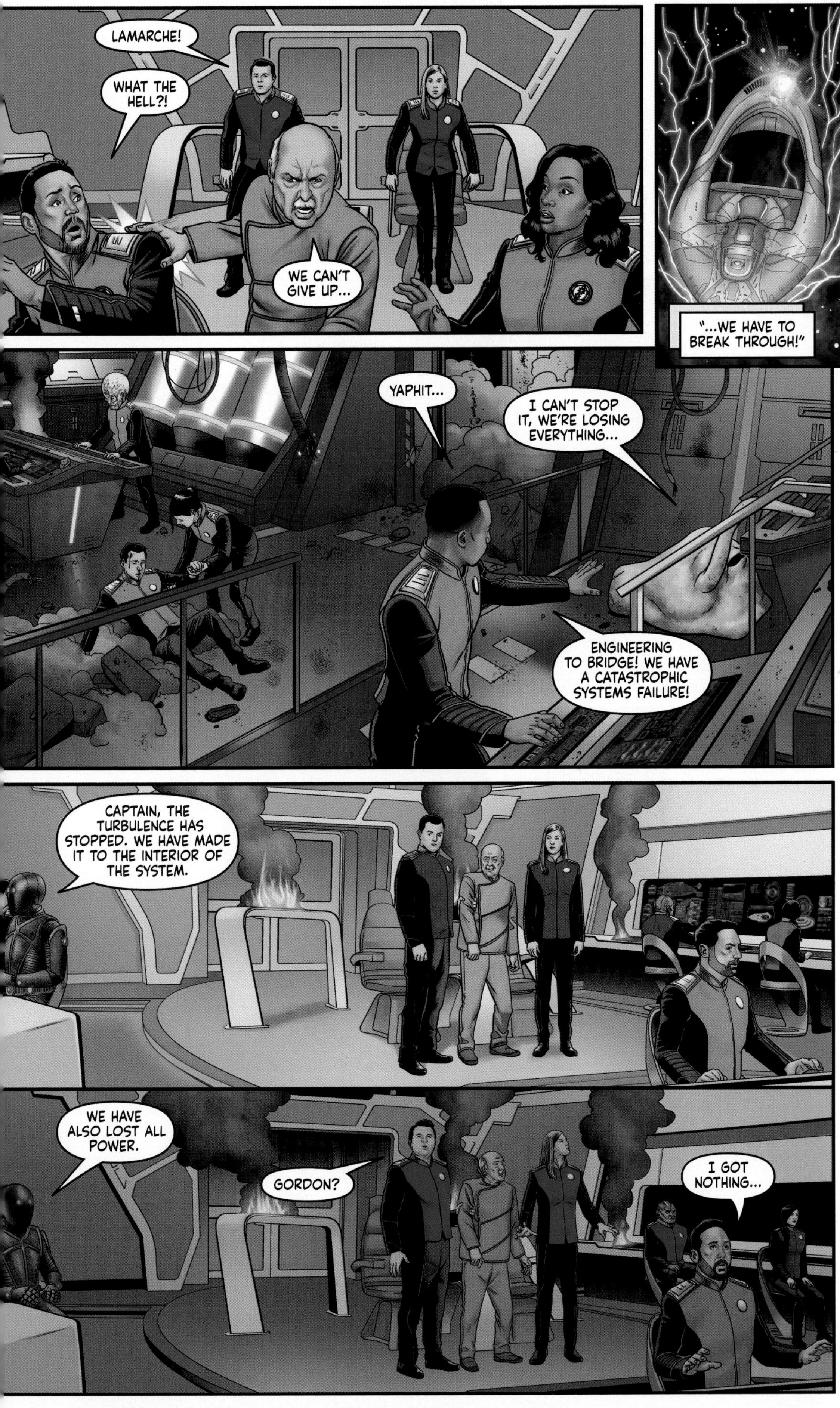
LAMARCHE!
WHAT THE HELL?!
WE CAN'T GIVE UP...
"...WE HAVE TO BREAK THROUGH!"
YAPHIT...
I CAN'T STOP IT, WE'RE LOSING EVERYTHING...
ENGINEERING TO BRIDGE! WE HAVE A CATASTROPHIC SYSTEMS FAILURE!
CAPTAIN, THE TURBULENCE HAS STOPPED. WE HAVE MADE IT TO THE INTERIOR OF THE SYSTEM.
WE HAVE ALSO LOST ALL POWER.
GORDON?
I GOT NOTHING...

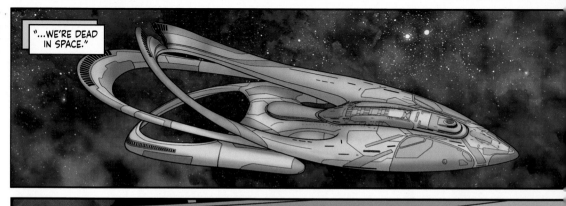

"...WE'RE DEAD IN SPACE."

ENGINEERING, TRY TO GET US SOME POWER AS SOON AS YOU CAN.

WE'RE WORKING ON IT.

BRIDGE TO SICKBAY, CASUALTY REPORT.

SIXTEEN INJURIES. THREE CONFIRMED DEATHS, THERE MAY BE MORE...

WHAT THE HELL DID YOU THINK YOU WERE DOING?

I'M SORRY... I JUST WANTED TO... I DIDN'T WANT ANYONE TO GET HURT.

A LITTLE LATE.

TAKE HIM TO THE BRIG.

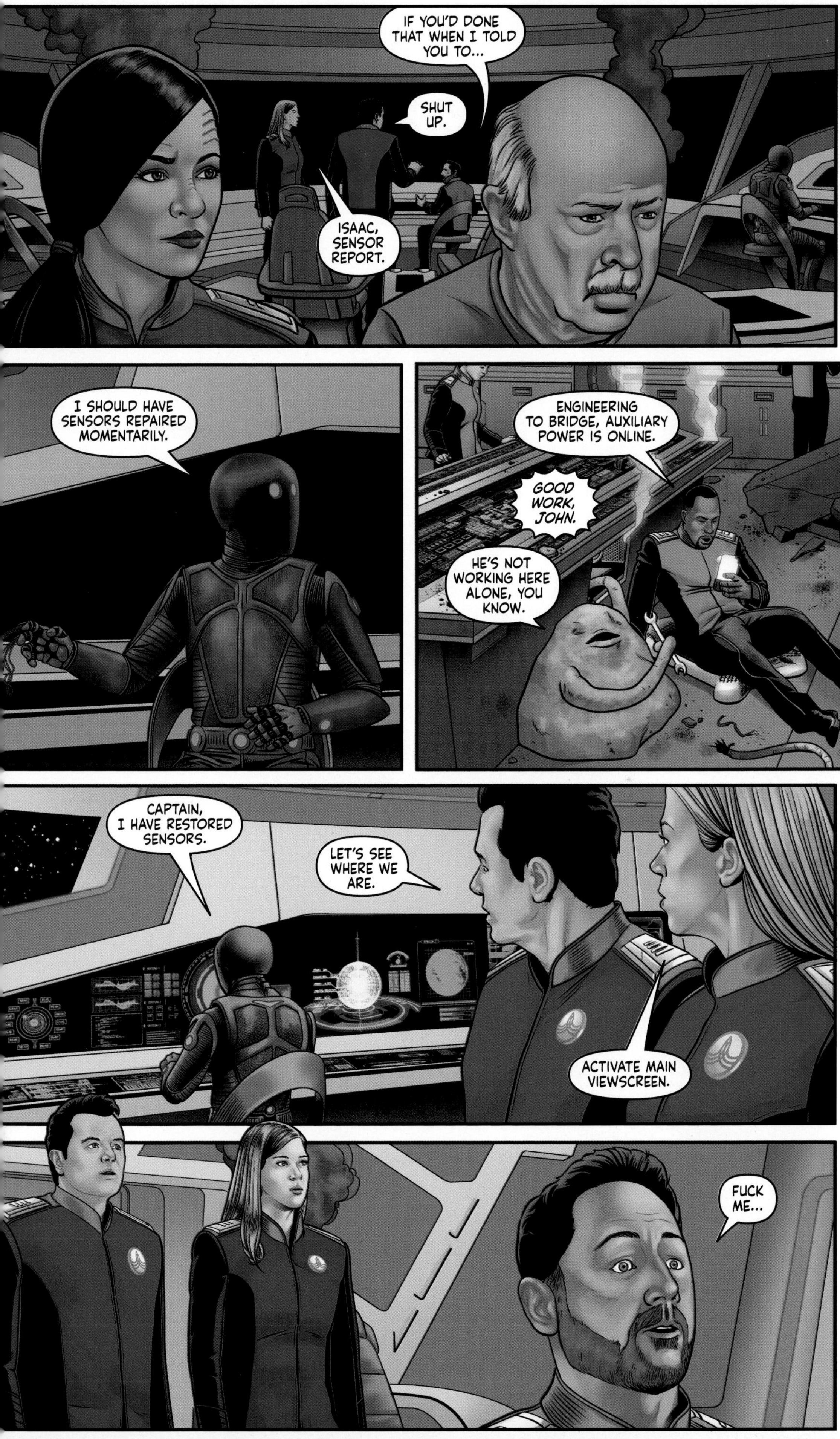
IF YOU'D DONE THAT WHEN I TOLD YOU TO...
SHUT UP.
ISAAC, SENSOR REPORT.
I SHOULD HAVE SENSORS REPAIRED MOMENTARILY.
ENGINEERING TO BRIDGE, AUXILIARY POWER IS ONLINE.
GOOD WORK, JOHN.
HE'S NOT WORKING HERE ALONE, YOU KNOW.
CAPTAIN, I HAVE RESTORED SENSORS.
LET'S SEE WHERE WE ARE.
ACTIVATE MAIN VIEWSCREEN.
FUCK ME...

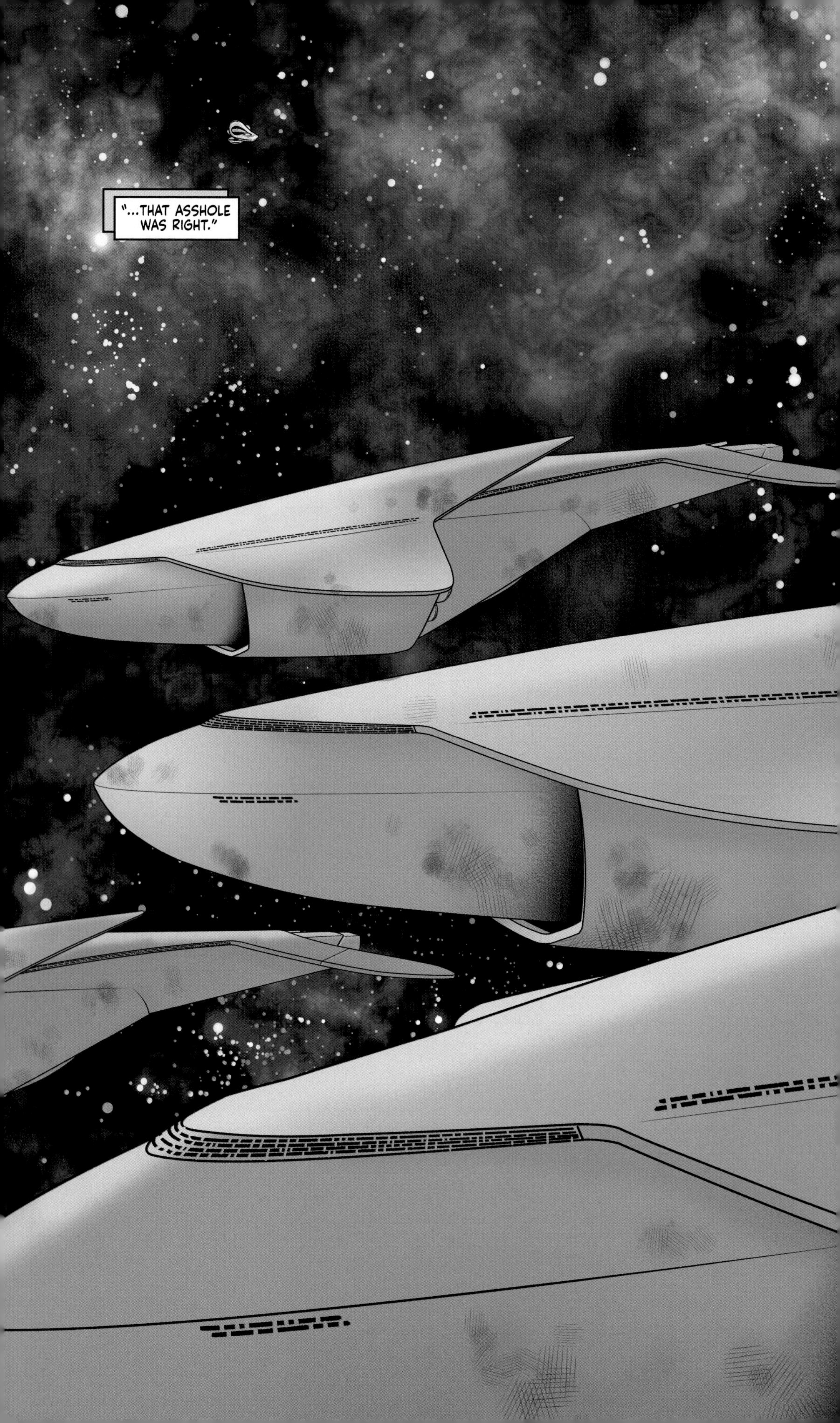
"...THAT ASSHOLE WAS RIGHT."

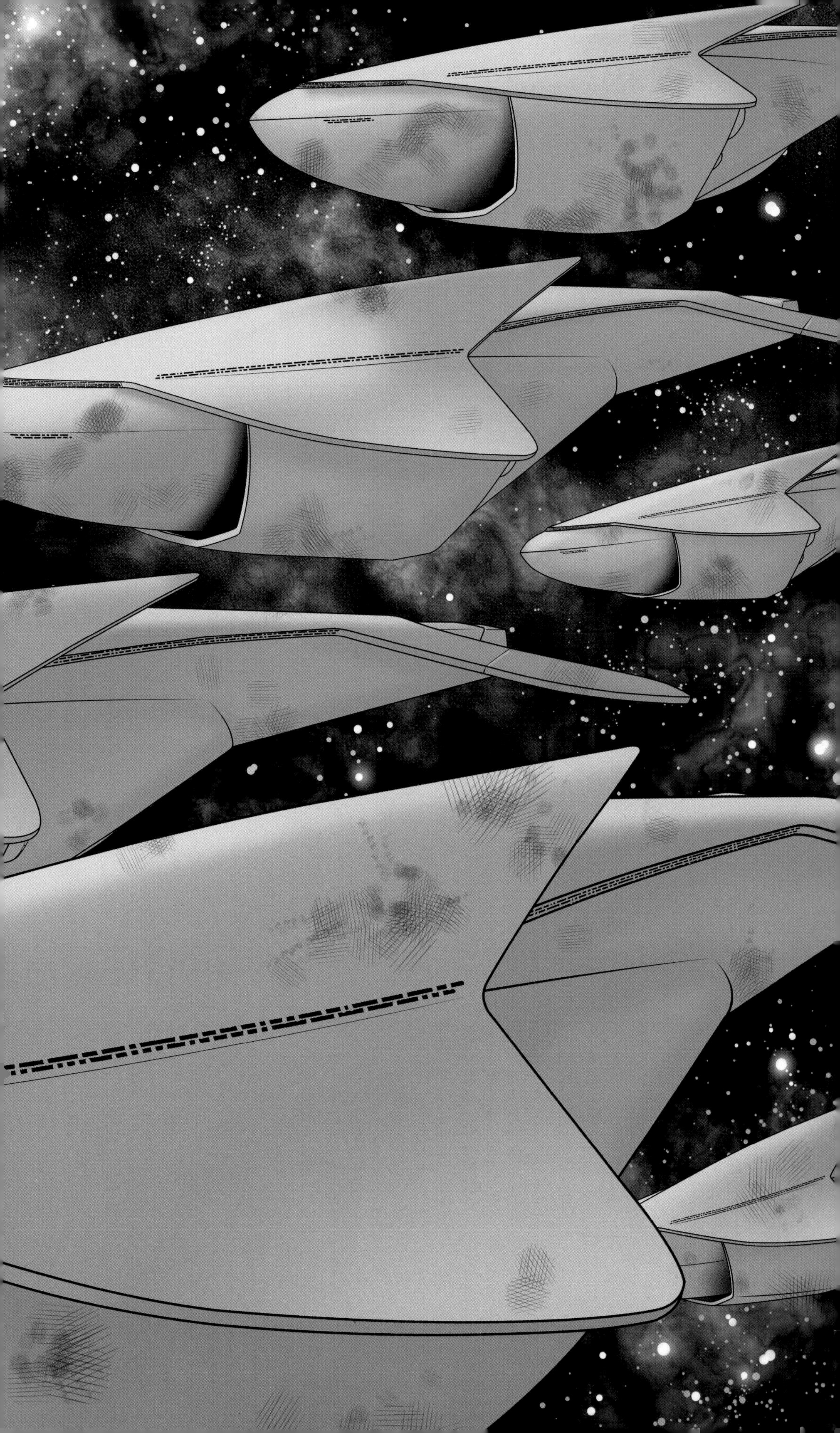

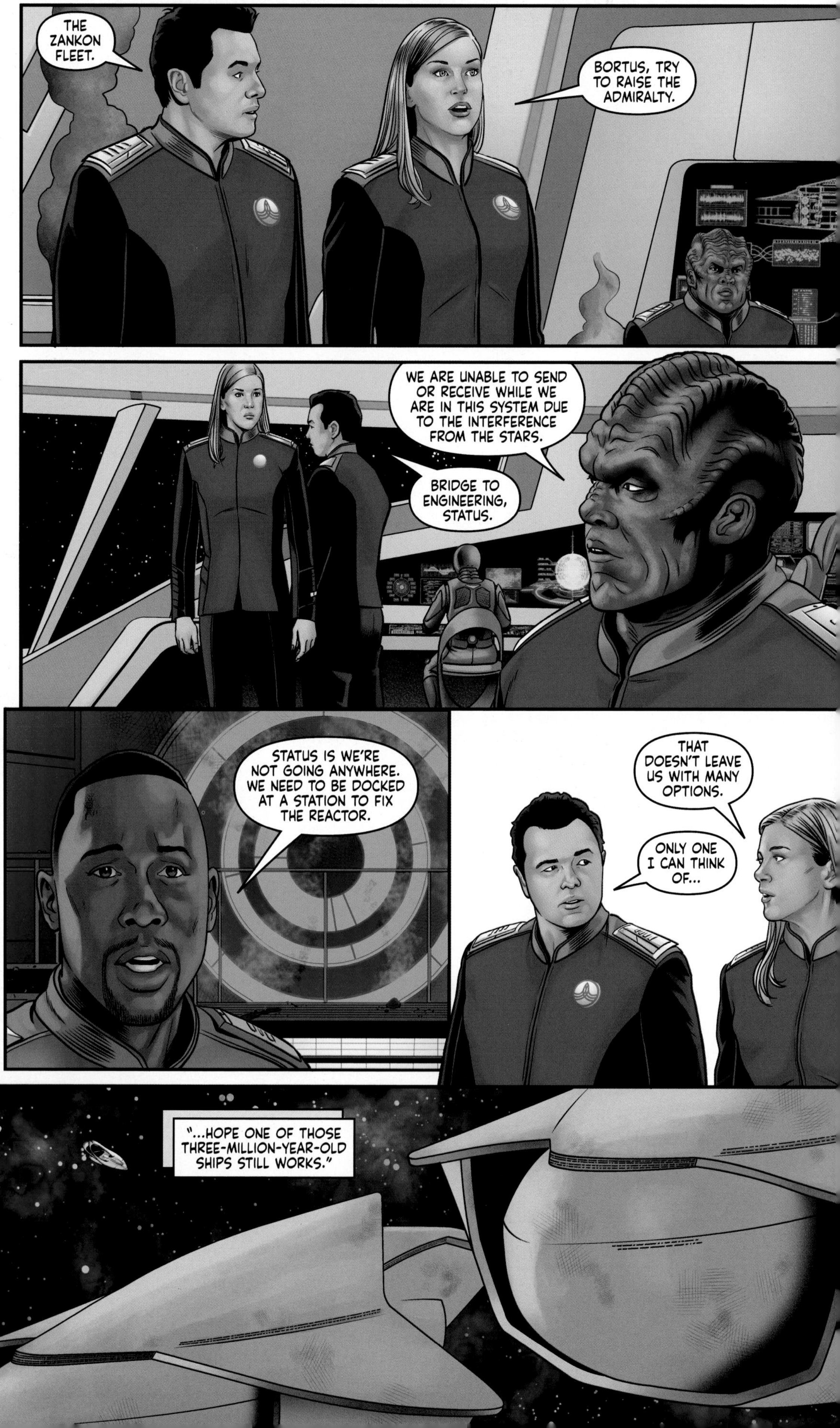
THE ZANKON FLEET.
BORTUS, TRY TO RAISE THE ADMIRALTY.
WE ARE UNABLE TO SEND OR RECEIVE WHILE WE ARE IN THIS SYSTEM DUE TO THE INTERFERENCE FROM THE STARS.
BRIDGE TO ENGINEERING, STATUS.
STATUS IS WE'RE NOT GOING ANYWHERE. WE NEED TO BE DOCKED AT A STATION TO FIX THE REACTOR.
THAT DOESN'T LEAVE US WITH MANY OPTIONS.
ONLY ONE I CAN THINK OF...
"...HOPE ONE OF THOSE THREE-MILLION-YEAR-OLD SHIPS STILL WORKS."

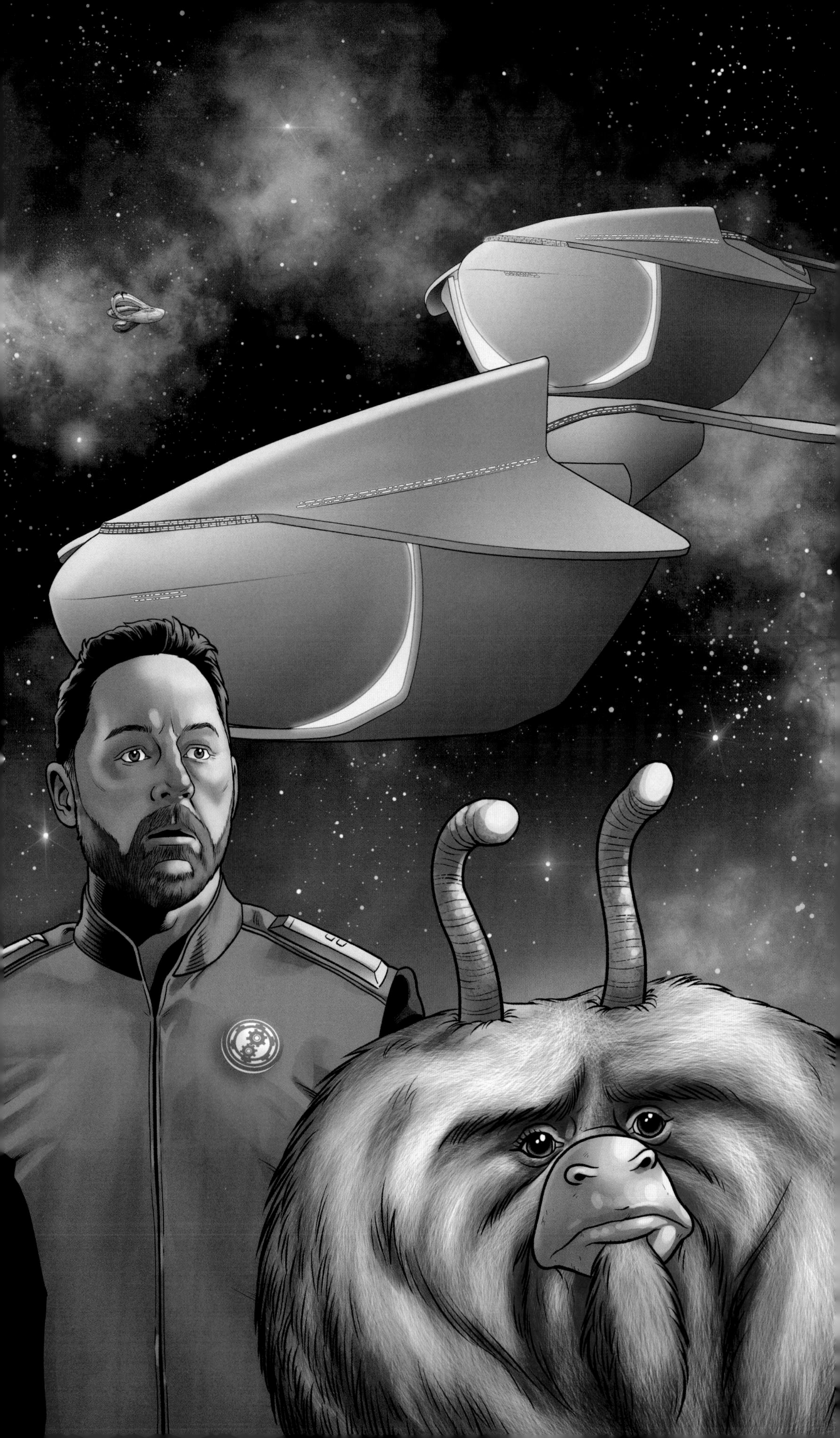

ARTIFACTS PART 2

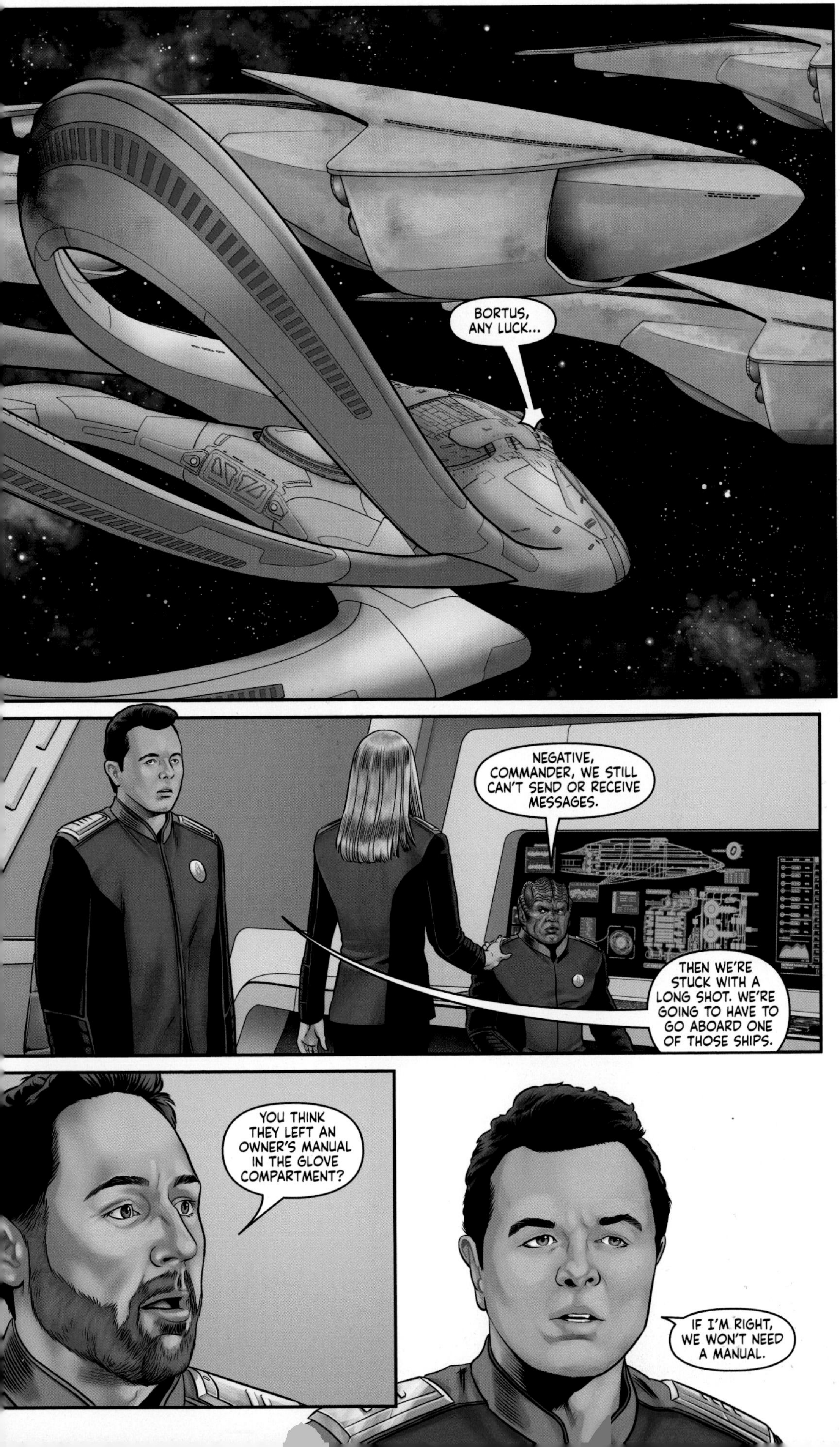
BORTUS, ANY LUCK...
NEGATIVE, COMMANDER, WE STILL CAN'T SEND OR RECEIVE MESSAGES.
THEN WE'RE STUCK WITH A LONG SHOT. WE'RE GOING TO HAVE TO GO ABOARD ONE OF THOSE SHIPS.
YOU THINK THEY LEFT AN OWNER'S MANUAL IN THE GLOVE COMPARTMENT?
IF I'M RIGHT, WE WON'T NEED A MANUAL.

YES, I CAN OPERATE ONE OF THOSE SHIPS. BUT YOU HAVE TO GET ME ABOARD.

MAYBE IT'S BETTER IF YOU JUST TELL US HOW, AND WE KEEP YOU HERE.

THAT WON'T WORK.

WHY NOT?

IF I TOLD YOU, I'D GIVE UP WHATEVER LEVERAGE I HAVE.

THIS IS NOT A GAME. THREE OF MY CREW ARE DEAD BECAUSE OF YOU. YOU'RE GOING TO FACE THE CONSEQUENCES.

I KNOW. BUT I BRING BACK [...] ONE OF THES[...] SHIPS, MAYBE [...] WILL LESSEN T[...] SEVERITY OF T[...] CONSEQUENCE[...]

DON'T COUNT ON IT.

WE'LL LEAVE IN AN HOUR.

I WILL NEED MY ASSISTANT.

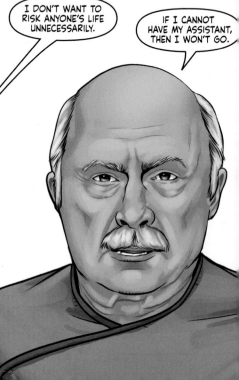

I DON'T WANT TO RISK ANYONE'S LIFE UNNECESSARILY.

IF I CANNOT HAVE MY ASSISTANT, THEN I WON'T GO.

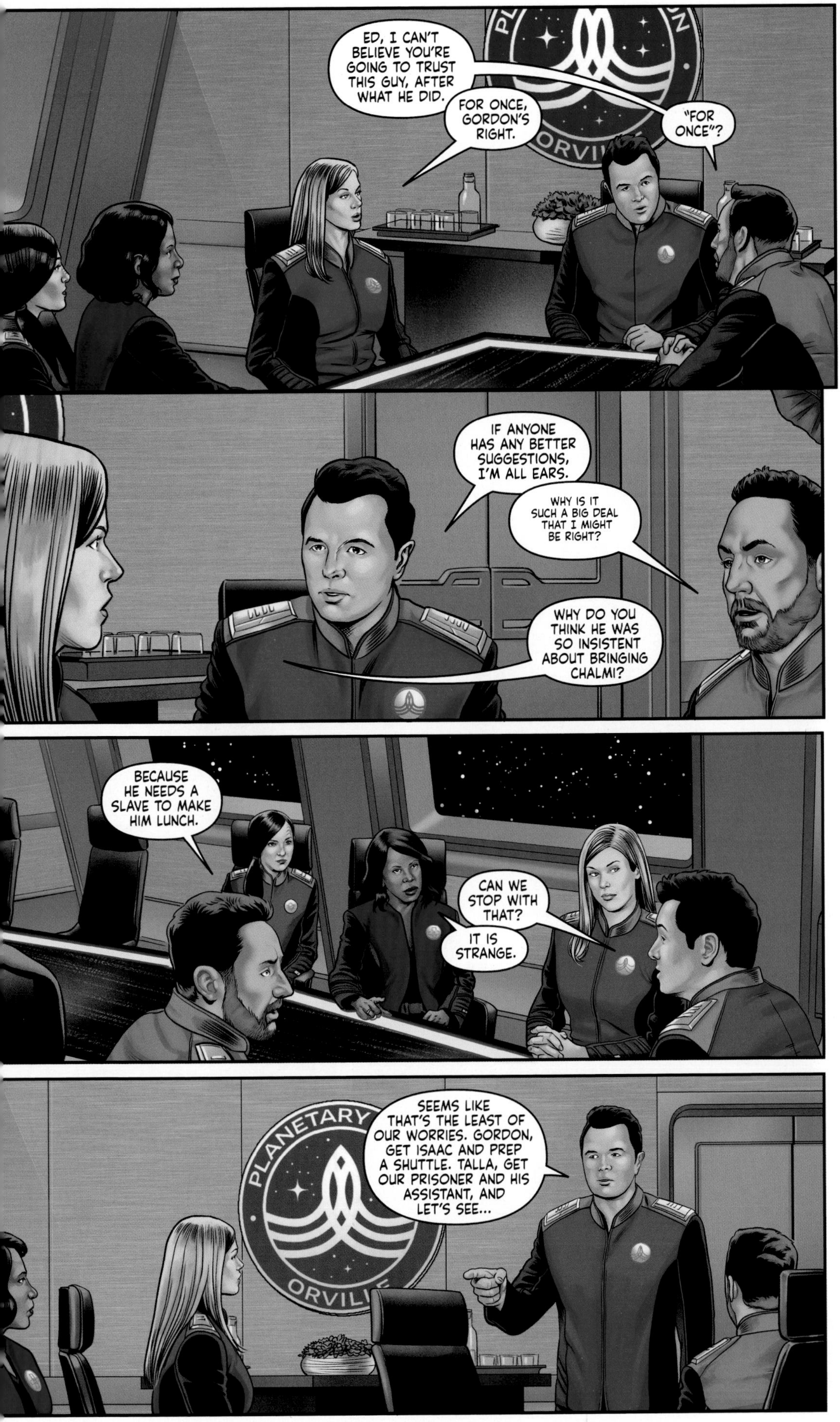
ED, I CAN'T BELIEVE YOU'RE GOING TO TRUST THIS GUY, AFTER WHAT HE DID.
FOR ONCE, GORDON'S RIGHT.
"FOR ONCE"?
IF ANYONE HAS ANY BETTER SUGGESTIONS, I'M ALL EARS.
WHY IS IT SUCH A BIG DEAL THAT I MIGHT BE RIGHT?
WHY DO YOU THINK HE WAS SO INSISTENT ABOUT BRINGING CHALMI?
BECAUSE HE NEEDS A SLAVE TO MAKE HIM LUNCH.
CAN WE STOP WITH THAT?
IT IS STRANGE.
SEEMS LIKE THAT'S THE LEAST OF OUR WORRIES. GORDON, GET ISAAC AND PREP A SHUTTLE. TALLA, GET OUR PRISONER AND HIS ASSISTANT, AND LET'S SEE...
PLANETARY
ORVILLE

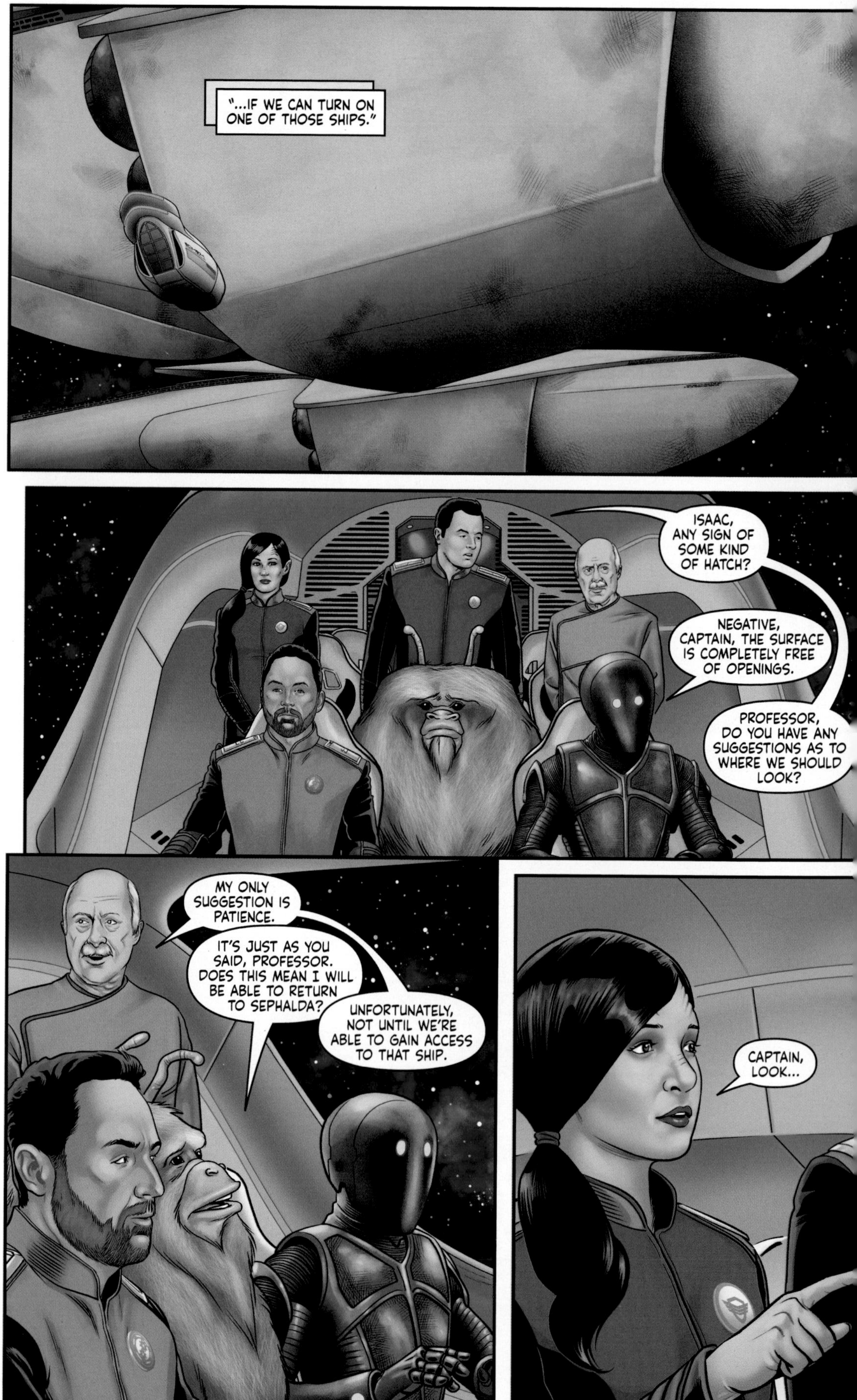
"...IF WE CAN TURN ON ONE OF THOSE SHIPS."
ISAAC, ANY SIGN OF SOME KIND OF HATCH?
NEGATIVE, CAPTAIN, THE SURFACE IS COMPLETELY FREE OF OPENINGS.
PROFESSOR, DO YOU HAVE ANY SUGGESTIONS AS TO WHERE WE SHOULD LOOK?
MY ONLY SUGGESTION IS PATIENCE.
IT'S JUST AS YOU SAID, PROFESSOR. DOES THIS MEAN I WILL BE ABLE TO RETURN TO SEPHALDA?
UNFORTUNATELY, NOT UNTIL WE'RE ABLE TO GAIN ACCESS TO THAT SHIP.
CAPTAIN, LOOK...

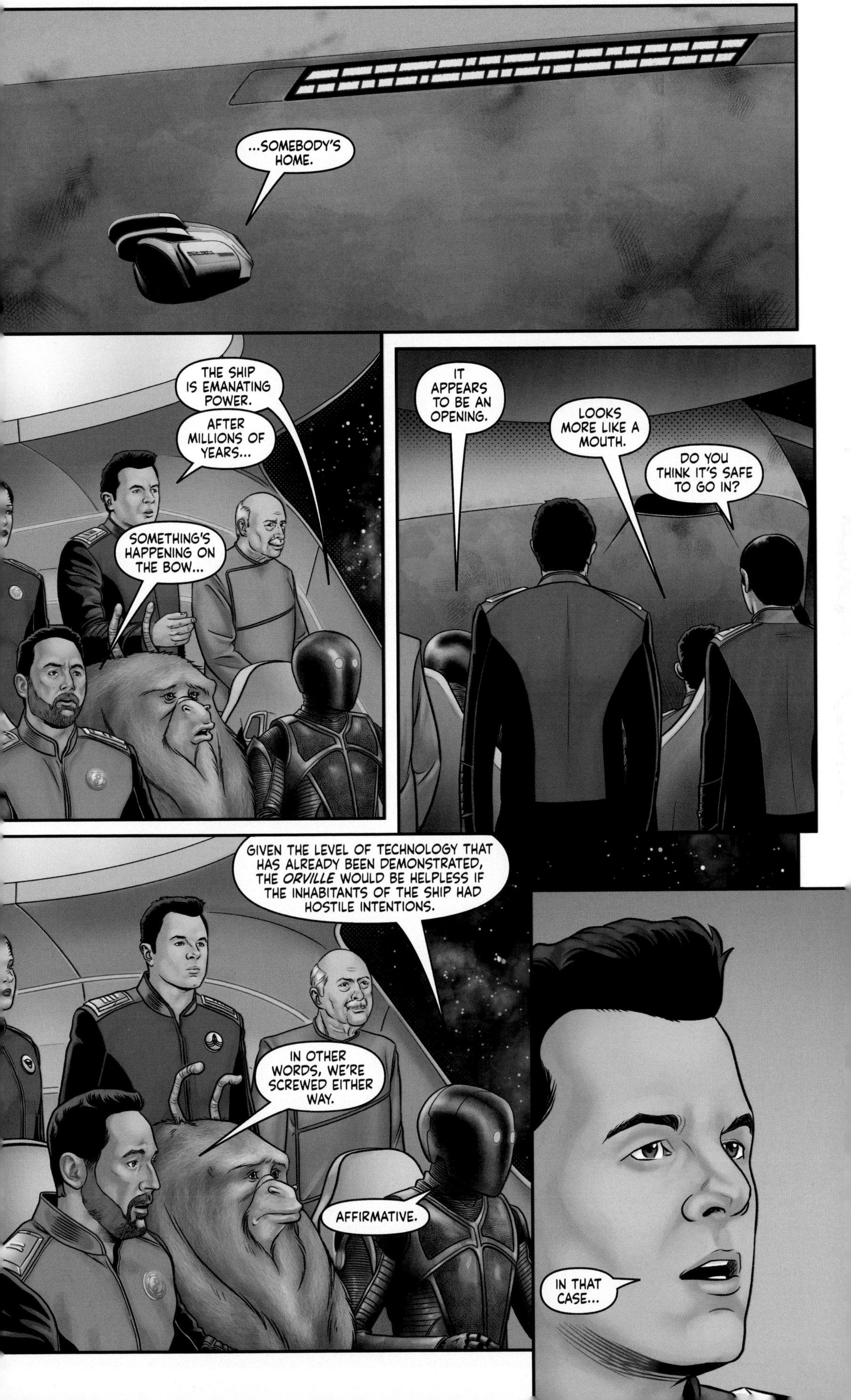
...SOMEBODY'S HOME.
THE SHIP IS EMANATING POWER.
AFTER MILLIONS OF YEARS...
SOMETHING'S HAPPENING ON THE BOW...
IT APPEARS TO BE AN OPENING.
LOOKS MORE LIKE A MOUTH.
DO YOU THINK IT'S SAFE TO GO IN?
GIVEN THE LEVEL OF TECHNOLOGY THAT HAS ALREADY BEEN DEMONSTRATED, THE *ORVILLE* WOULD BE HELPLESS IF THE INHABITANTS OF THE SHIP HAD HOSTILE INTENTIONS.
IN OTHER WORDS, WE'RE SCREWED EITHER WAY.
AFFIRMATIVE.
IN THAT CASE...

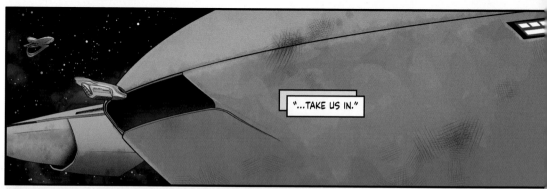

"...TAKE US IN."

"I FEEL LIKE WE'RE IN THAT STORY FROM THE BIBLE, ABOUT THE WHALE AND PINOCCHIO."

"GORDON, THAT'S NOT... FORGET IT."

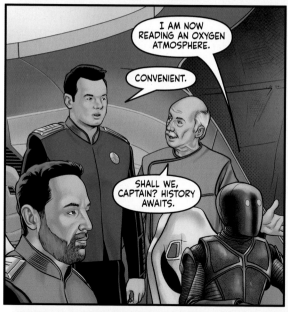

I AM NOW READING AN OXYGEN ATMOSPHERE.

CONVENIENT.

SHALL WE, CAPTAIN? HISTORY AWAITS.

IT FEELS LIKE HE'S EXPECTED ALL OF THIS. KEEP AN EYE ON HIM.

KIND OF GOES WITHOUT SAYING.

HOLY CRAP...

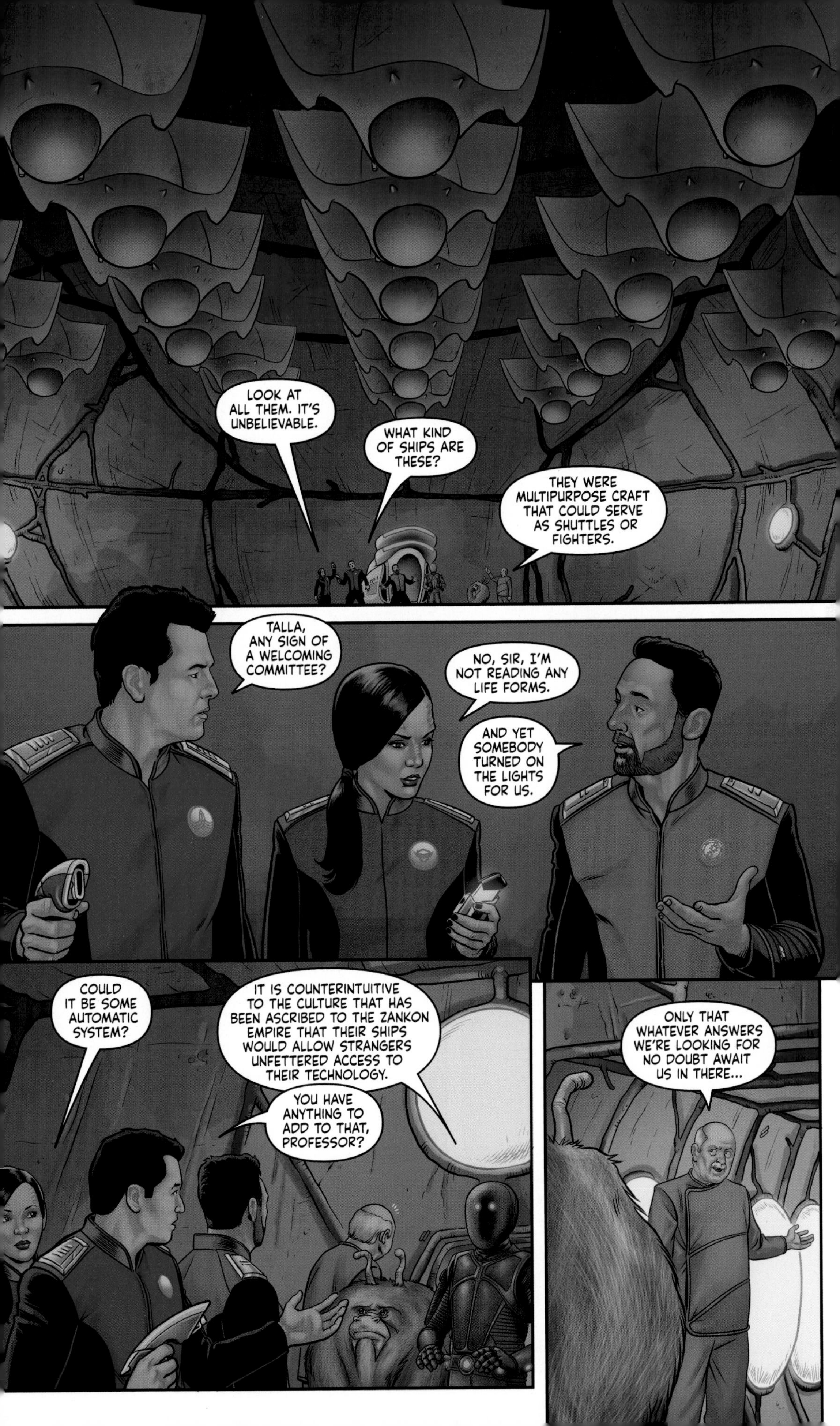
LOOK AT ALL THEM. IT'S UNBELIEVABLE.
WHAT KIND OF SHIPS ARE THESE?
THEY WERE MULTIPURPOSE CRAFT THAT COULD SERVE AS SHUTTLES OR FIGHTERS.
TALLA, ANY SIGN OF A WELCOMING COMMITTEE?
NO, SIR, I'M NOT READING ANY LIFE FORMS.
AND YET SOMEBODY TURNED ON THE LIGHTS FOR US.
COULD IT BE SOME AUTOMATIC SYSTEM?
IT IS COUNTERINTUITIVE TO THE CULTURE THAT HAS BEEN ASCRIBED TO THE ZANKON EMPIRE THAT THEIR SHIPS WOULD ALLOW STRANGERS UNFETTERED ACCESS TO THEIR TECHNOLOGY.
YOU HAVE ANYTHING TO ADD TO THAT, PROFESSOR?
ONLY THAT WHATEVER ANSWERS WE'RE LOOKING FOR NO DOUBT AWAIT US IN THERE...

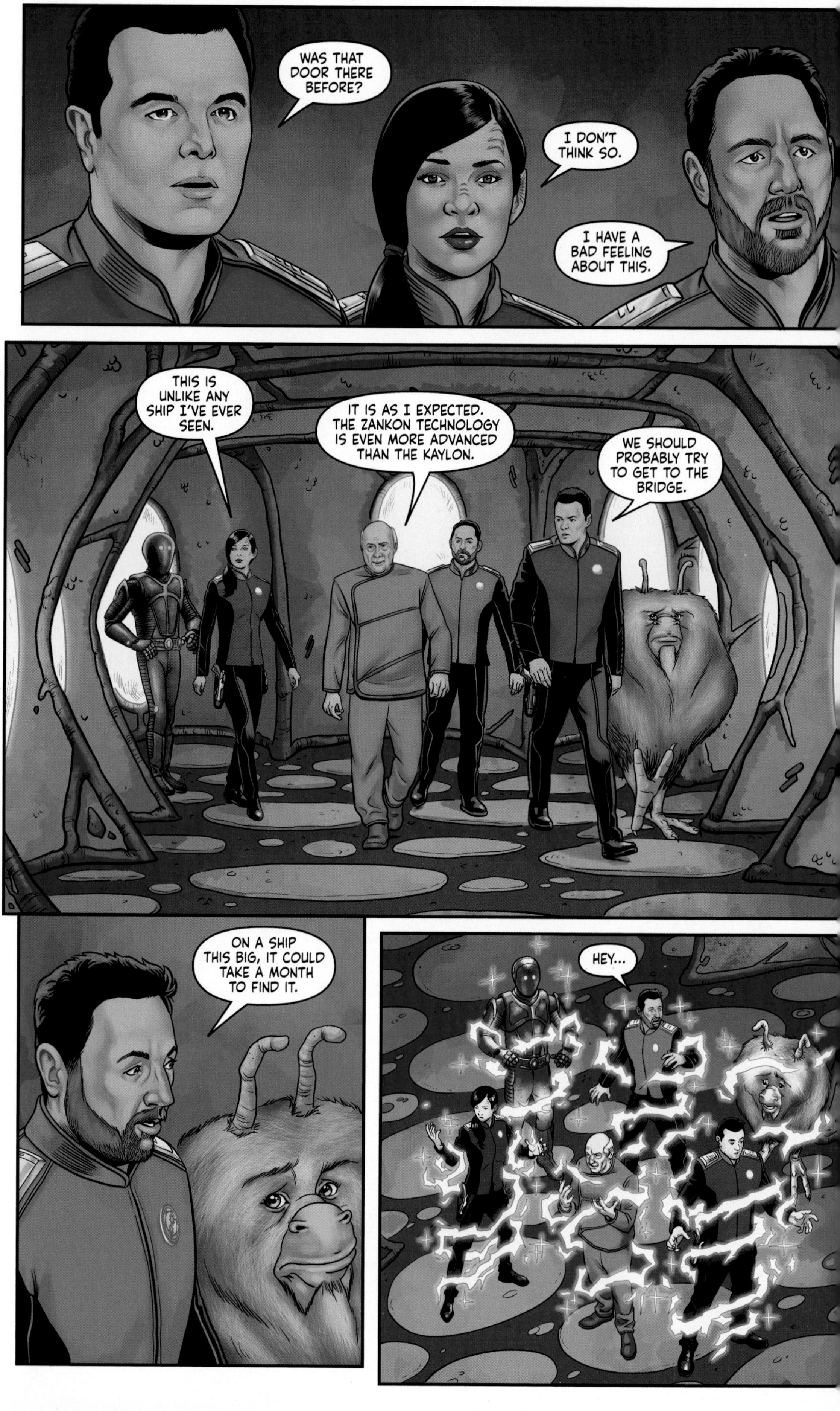
WAS THAT DOOR THERE BEFORE?
I DON'T THINK SO.
I HAVE A BAD FEELING ABOUT THIS.
THIS IS UNLIKE ANY SHIP I'VE EVER SEEN.
IT IS AS I EXPECTED. THE ZANKON TECHNOLOGY IS EVEN MORE ADVANCED THAN THE KAYLON.
WE SHOULD PROBABLY TRY TO GET TO THE BRIDGE.
ON A SHIP THIS BIG, IT COULD TAKE A MONTH TO FIND IT.
HEY...

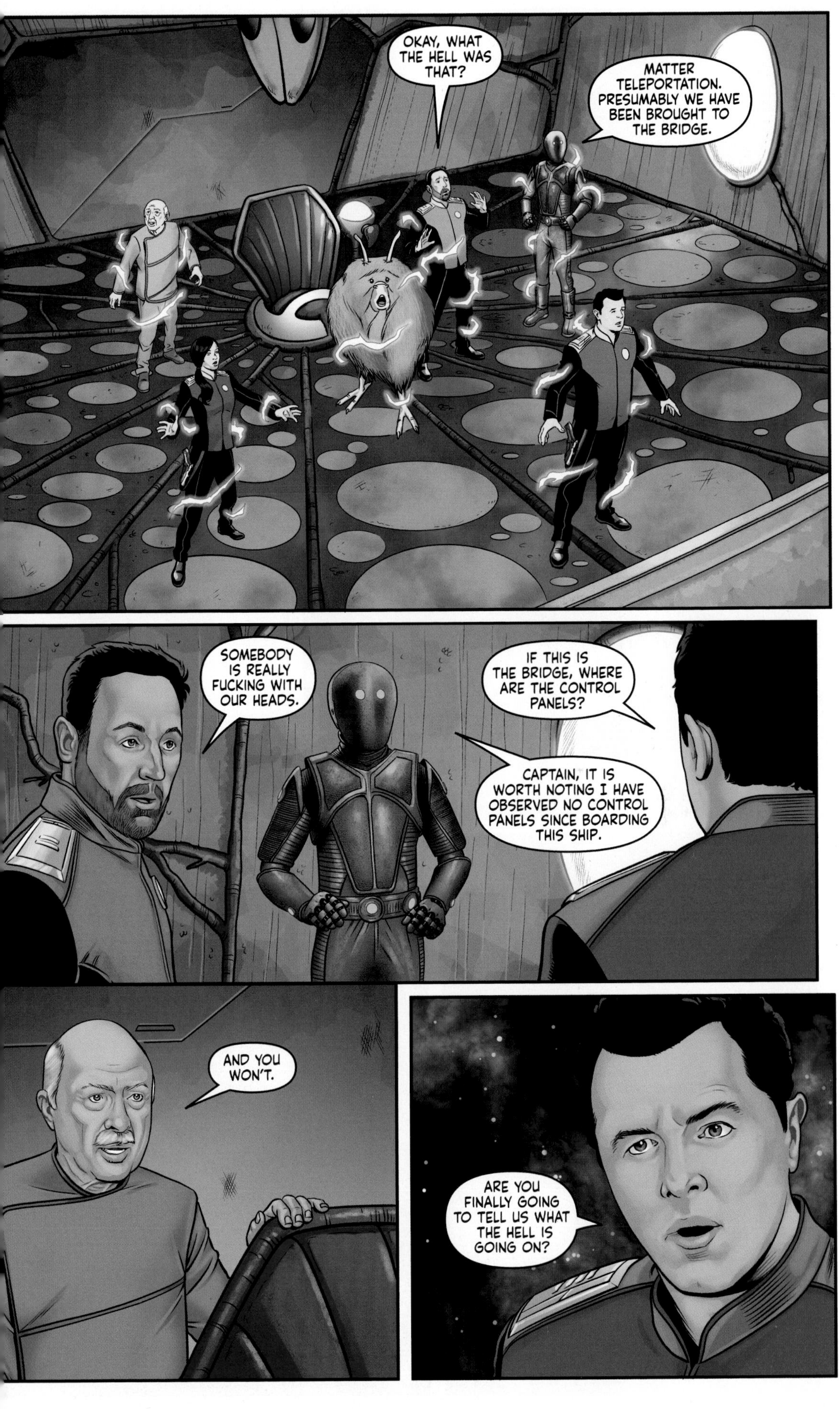
OKAY, WHAT THE HELL WAS THAT?
MATTER TELEPORTATION. PRESUMABLY WE HAVE BEEN BROUGHT TO THE BRIDGE.
SOMEBODY IS REALLY FUCKING WITH OUR HEADS.
IF THIS IS THE BRIDGE, WHERE ARE THE CONTROL PANELS?
CAPTAIN, IT IS WORTH NOTING I HAVE OBSERVED NO CONTROL PANELS SINCE BOARDING THIS SHIP.
AND YOU WON'T.
ARE YOU FINALLY GOING TO TELL US WHAT THE HELL IS GOING ON?

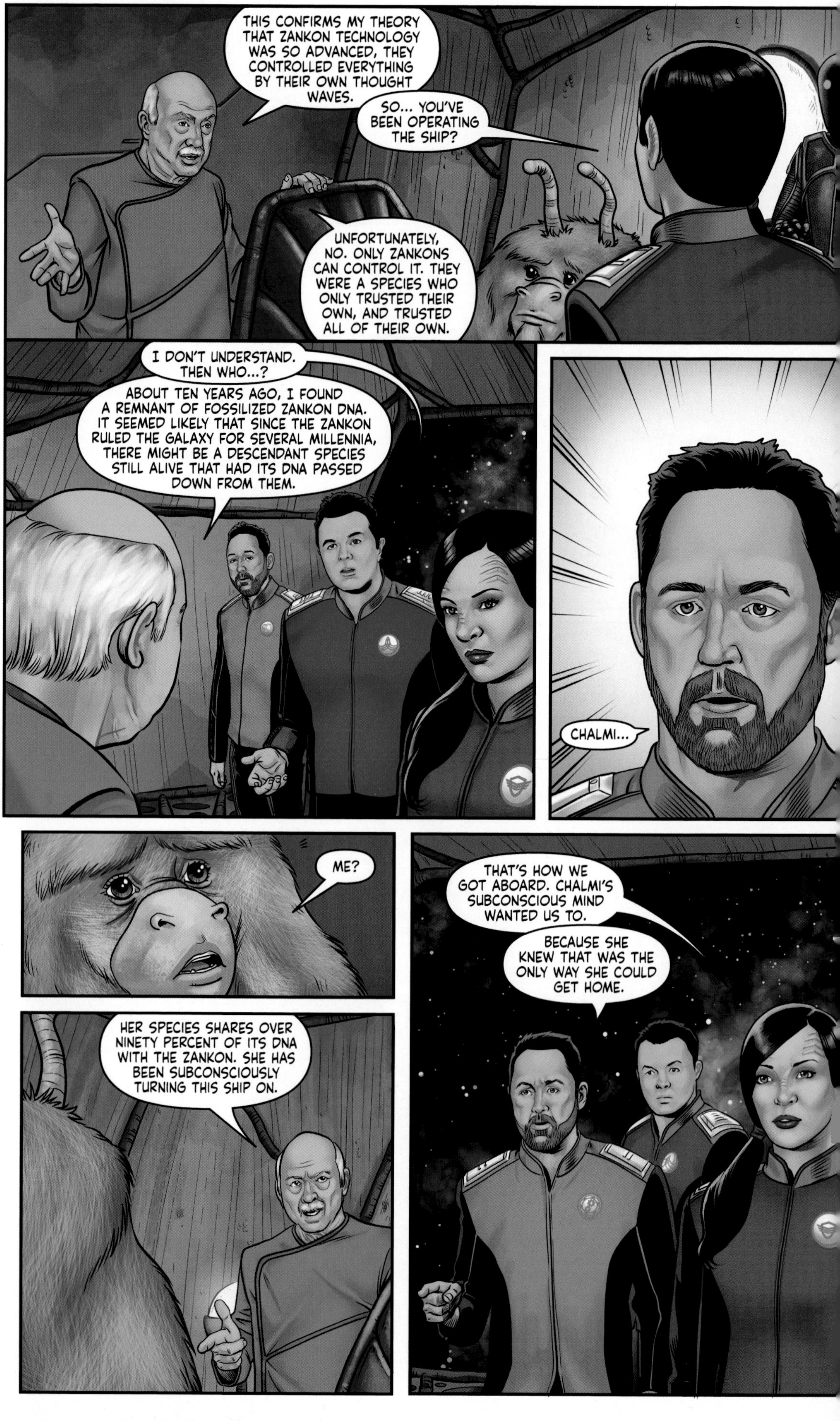
THIS CONFIRMS MY THEORY THAT ZANKON TECHNOLOGY WAS SO ADVANCED, THEY CONTROLLED EVERYTHING BY THEIR OWN THOUGHT WAVES.
SO... YOU'VE BEEN OPERATING THE SHIP?
UNFORTUNATELY, NO. ONLY ZANKONS CAN CONTROL IT. THEY WERE A SPECIES WHO ONLY TRUSTED THEIR OWN, AND TRUSTED ALL OF THEIR OWN.
I DON'T UNDERSTAND. THEN WHO...?
ABOUT TEN YEARS AGO, I FOUND A REMNANT OF FOSSILIZED ZANKON DNA. IT SEEMED LIKELY THAT SINCE THE ZANKON RULED THE GALAXY FOR SEVERAL MILLENNIA, THERE MIGHT BE A DESCENDANT SPECIES STILL ALIVE THAT HAD ITS DNA PASSED DOWN FROM THEM.
CHALMI...
ME?
HER SPECIES SHARES OVER NINETY PERCENT OF ITS DNA WITH THE ZANKON. SHE HAS BEEN SUBCONSCIOUSLY TURNING THIS SHIP ON.
THAT'S HOW WE GOT ABOARD. CHALMI'S SUBCONSCIOUS MIND WANTED US TO.
BECAUSE SHE KNEW THAT WAS THE ONLY WAY SHE COULD GET HOME.

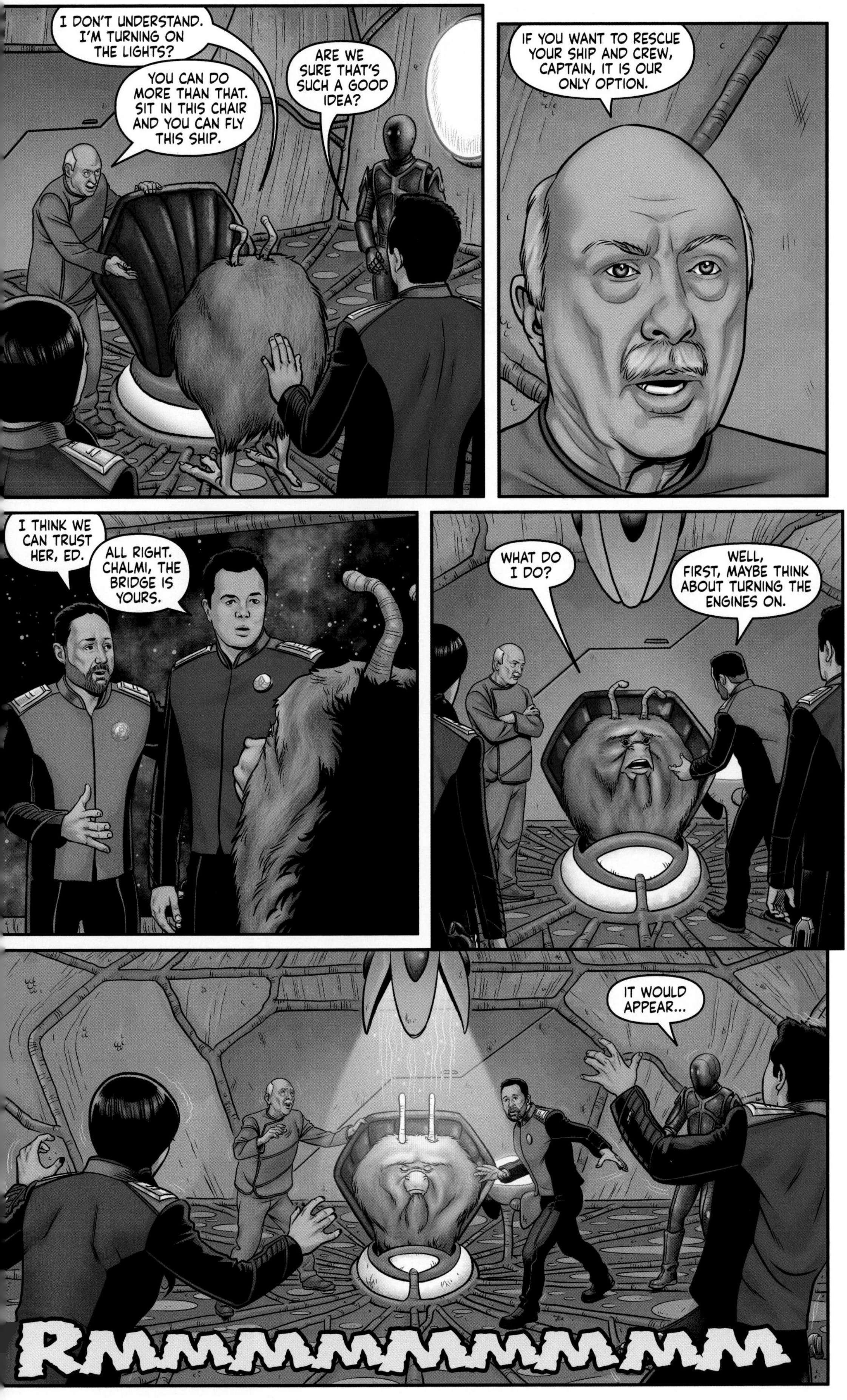

I DON'T UNDERSTAND. I'M TURNING ON THE LIGHTS?
YOU CAN DO MORE THAN THAT. SIT IN THIS CHAIR AND YOU CAN FLY THIS SHIP.
ARE WE SURE THAT'S SUCH A GOOD IDEA?
IF YOU WANT TO RESCUE YOUR SHIP AND CREW, CAPTAIN, IT IS OUR ONLY OPTION.
I THINK WE CAN TRUST HER, ED.
ALL RIGHT. CHALMI, THE BRIDGE IS YOURS.
WHAT DO I DO?
WELL, FIRST, MAYBE THINK ABOUT TURNING THE ENGINES ON.
IT WOULD APPEAR...
RMMMMMMMMMM

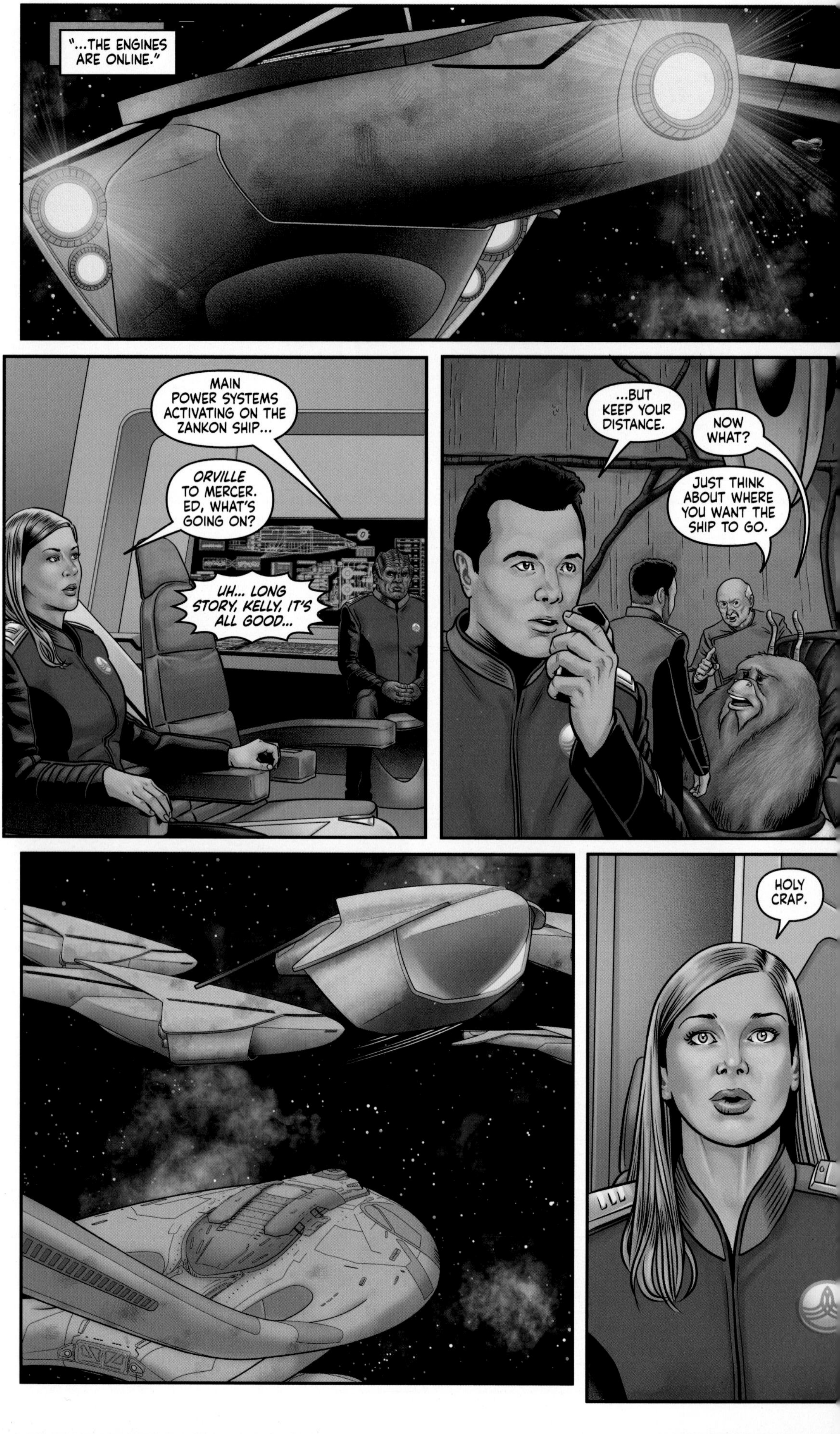
"...THE ENGINES ARE ONLINE."
MAIN POWER SYSTEMS ACTIVATING ON THE ZANKON SHIP...
ORVILLE TO MERCER. ED, WHAT'S GOING ON?
UH... LONG STORY, KELLY, IT'S ALL GOOD...
...BUT KEEP YOUR DISTANCE.
NOW WHAT?
JUST THINK ABOUT WHERE YOU WANT THE SHIP TO GO.
HOLY CRAP.

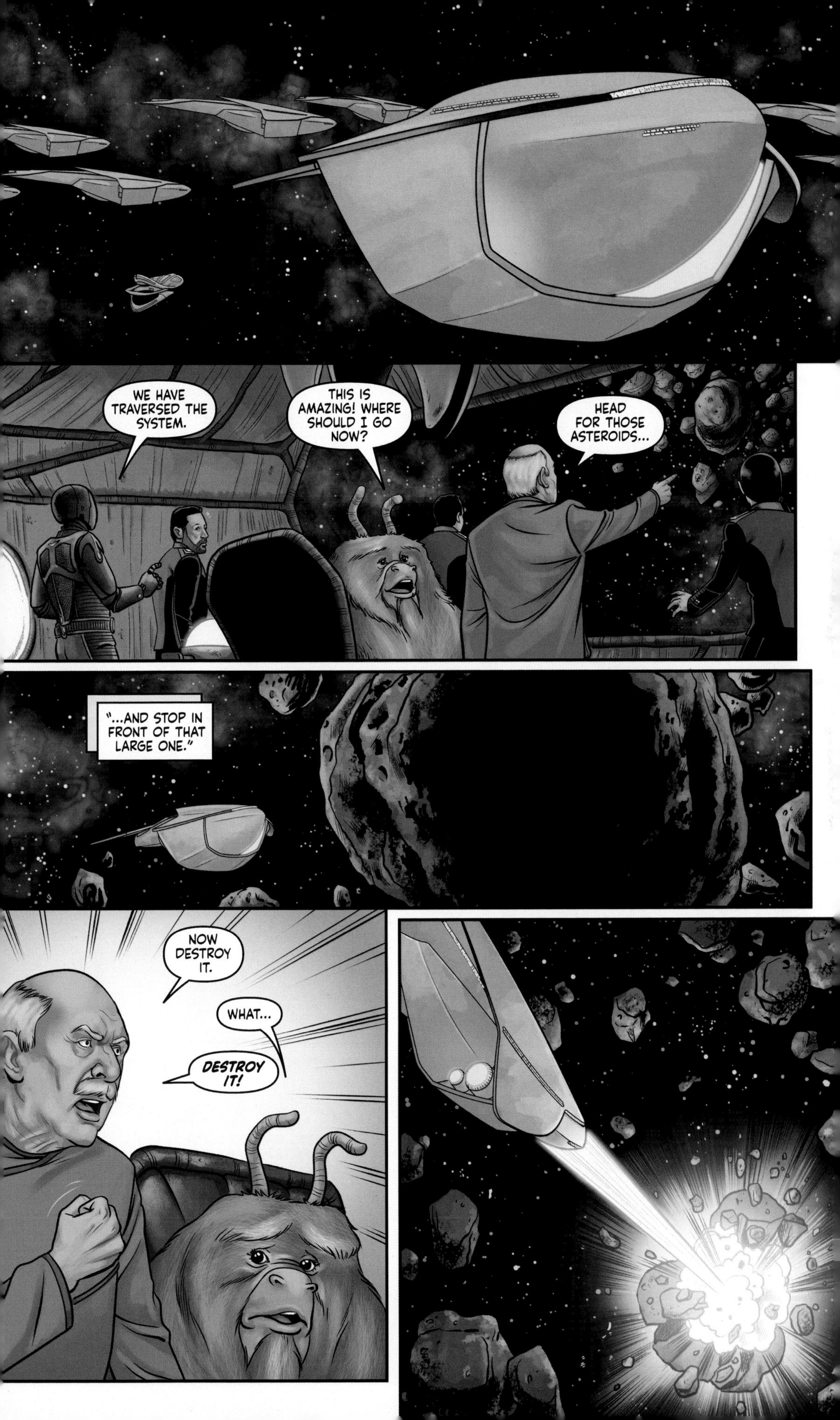
WE HAVE TRAVERSED THE SYSTEM.
THIS IS AMAZING! WHERE SHOULD I GO NOW?
HEAD FOR THOSE ASTEROIDS...
"...AND STOP IN FRONT OF THAT LARGE ONE."
NOW DESTROY IT.
WHAT...
DESTROY IT!

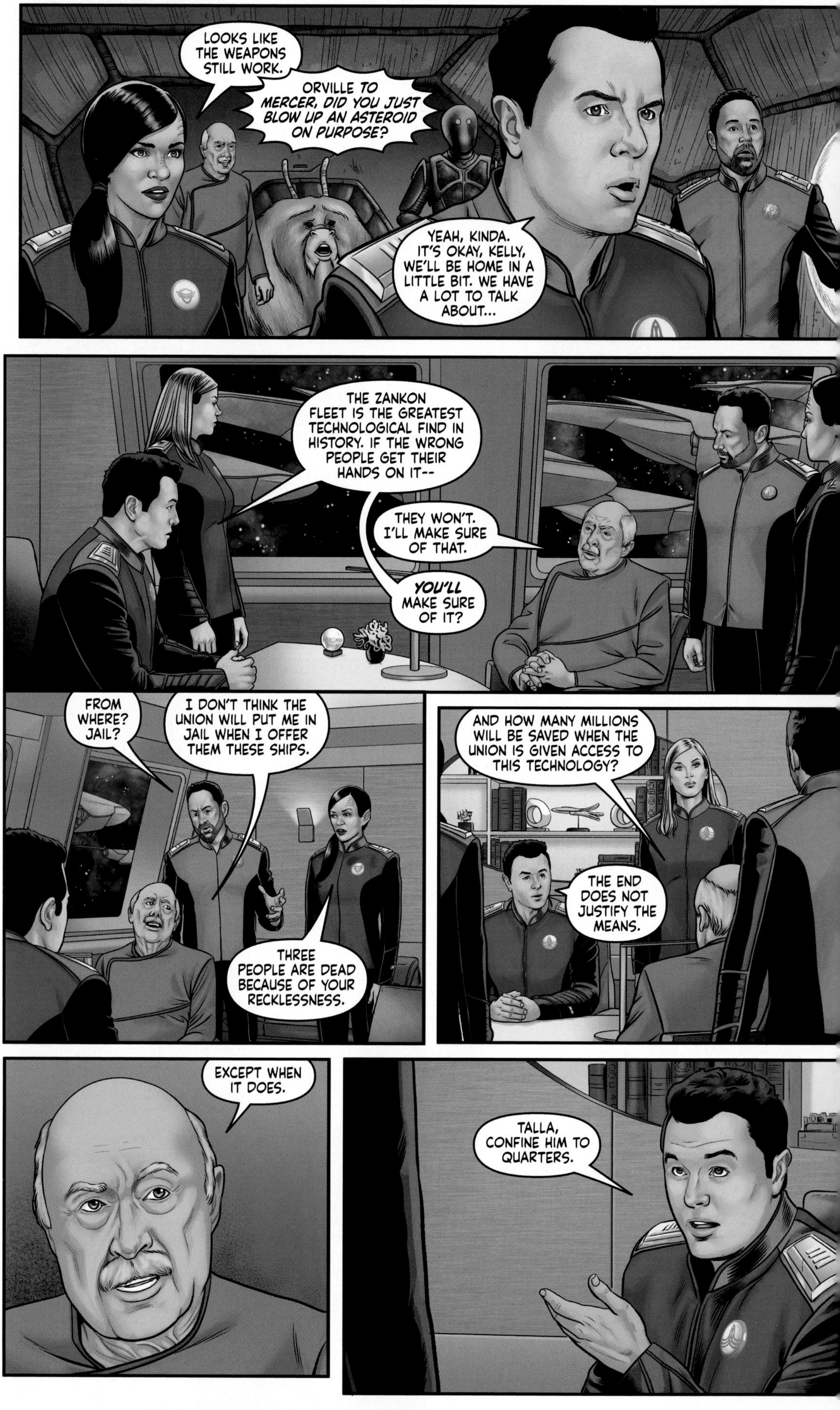
LOOKS LIKE THE WEAPONS STILL WORK.
ORVILLE TO MERCER, DID YOU JUST BLOW UP AN ASTEROID ON PURPOSE?
YEAH, KINDA. IT'S OKAY, KELLY, WE'LL BE HOME IN A LITTLE BIT. WE HAVE A LOT TO TALK ABOUT...
THE ZANKON FLEET IS THE GREATEST TECHNOLOGICAL FIND IN HISTORY. IF THE WRONG PEOPLE GET THEIR HANDS ON IT--
THEY WON'T. I'LL MAKE SURE OF THAT.
YOU'LL MAKE SURE OF IT?
FROM WHERE? JAIL?
I DON'T THINK THE UNION WILL PUT ME IN JAIL WHEN I OFFER THEM THESE SHIPS.
THREE PEOPLE ARE DEAD BECAUSE OF YOUR RECKLESSNESS.
AND HOW MANY MILLIONS WILL BE SAVED WHEN THE UNION IS GIVEN ACCESS TO THIS TECHNOLOGY?
THE END DOES NOT JUSTIFY THE MEANS.
EXCEPT WHEN IT DOES.
TALLA, CONFINE HIM TO QUARTERS.

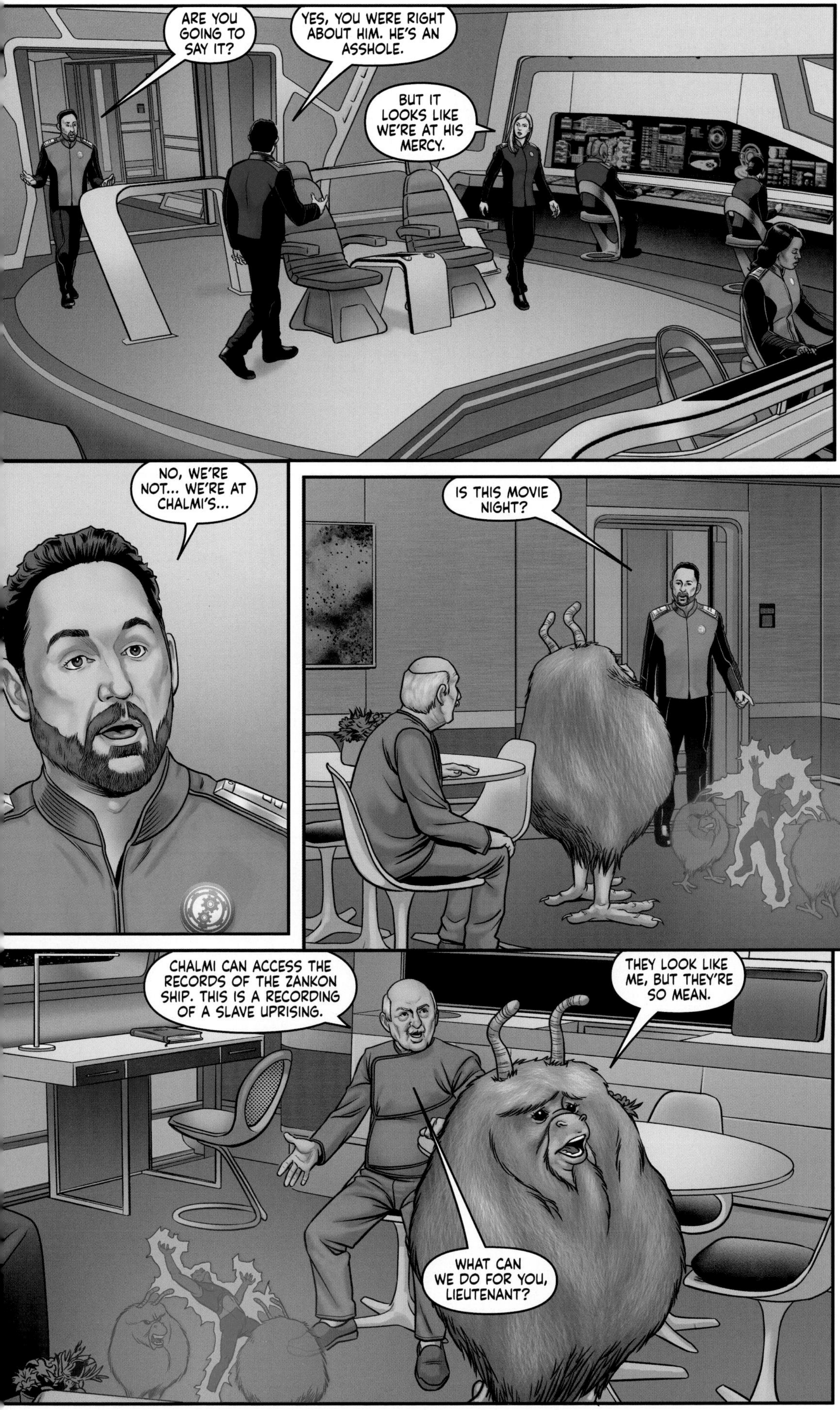
ARE YOU GOING TO SAY IT?
YES, YOU WERE RIGHT ABOUT HIM. HE'S AN ASSHOLE.
BUT IT LOOKS LIKE WE'RE AT HIS MERCY.
NO, WE'RE NOT... WE'RE AT CHALMI'S...
IS THIS MOVIE NIGHT?
CHALMI CAN ACCESS THE RECORDS OF THE ZANKON SHIP. THIS IS A RECORDING OF A SLAVE UPRISING.
THEY LOOK LIKE ME, BUT THEY'RE SO MEAN.
WHAT CAN WE DO FOR YOU, LIEUTENANT?

WELL, I WAS JUST WONDERING IF YOU'VE FILLED HER IN ON WHAT'S NEXT?

WE'RE GOING HOME.

YEAH, AND THEN WHAT?

I'M GOING TO HAVE TO ASK YOU TO LEAVE, LIEUTENANT...

MAKE ME.

HAS HE TOLD YOU HE'S GOING TO NEED A LOT MORE OF YOUR PEOPLE TO FLY THOSE SHIPS? HE'S NOT SATISFIED TURNING YOU INTO A SLAVE, CHALMI. HE WANTS ALL YOUR FRIENDS AND FAMILY TOO.

IS THIS... TRUE?

HE IS OVERSIMPLIFYING THIS TO UPSET YOU. WITH THESE SHIPS, CHALMI, YOU AND YOUR PEOPLE WILL BE THE MOST POWERFUL RACE IN THE GALAXY.

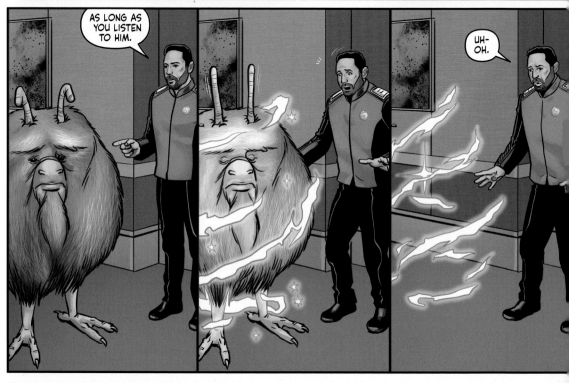

AS LONG AS YOU LISTEN TO HIM.

UH-OH.

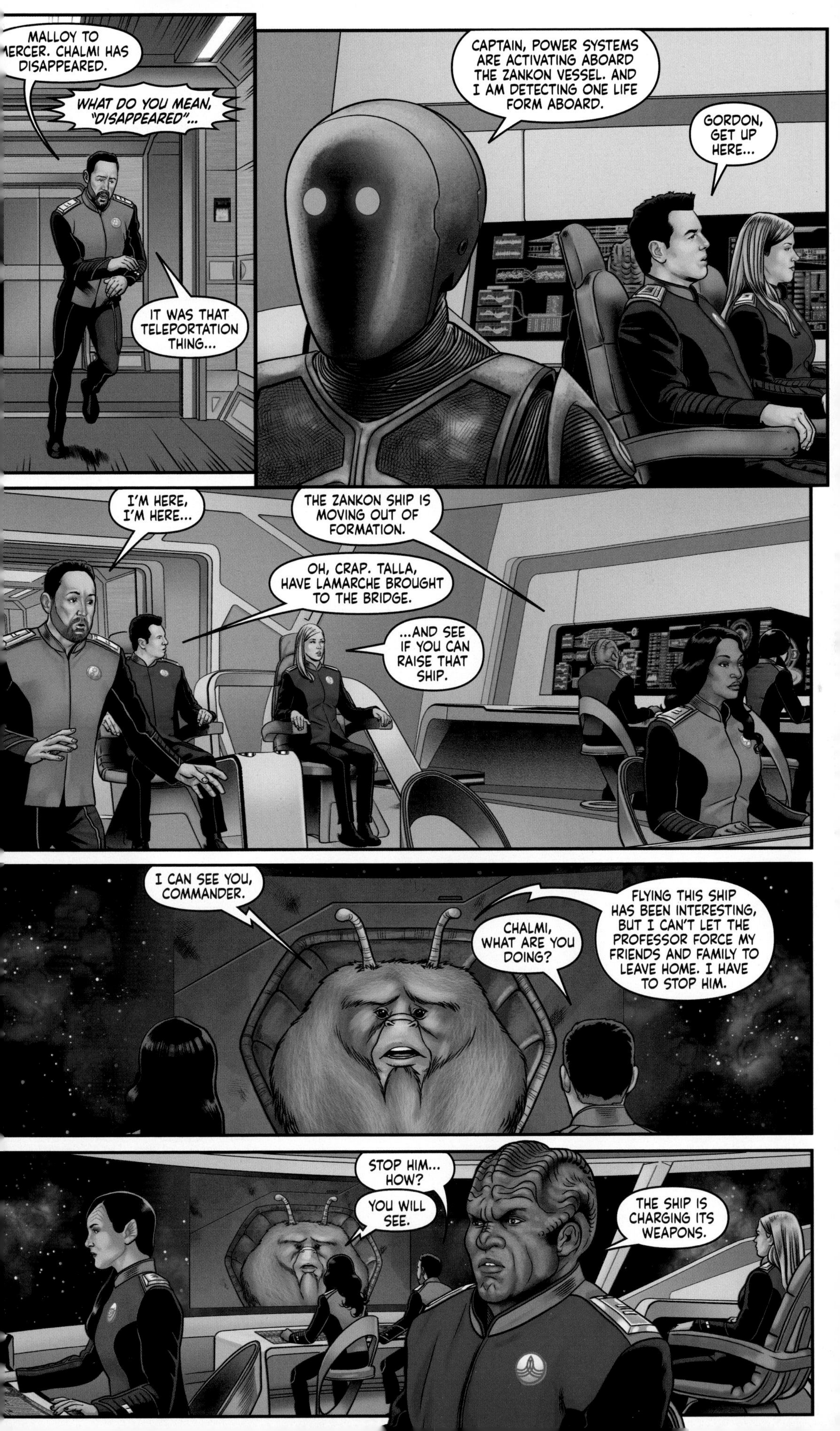
MALLOY TO MERCER. CHALMI HAS DISAPPEARED.
WHAT DO YOU MEAN, "DISAPPEARED"...
IT WAS THAT TELEPORTATION THING...
CAPTAIN, POWER SYSTEMS ARE ACTIVATING ABOARD THE ZANKON VESSEL. AND I AM DETECTING ONE LIFE FORM ABOARD.
GORDON, GET UP HERE...
I'M HERE, I'M HERE...
THE ZANKON SHIP IS MOVING OUT OF FORMATION.
OH, CRAP. TALLA, HAVE LAMARCHE BROUGHT TO THE BRIDGE.
...AND SEE IF YOU CAN RAISE THAT SHIP.
I CAN SEE YOU, COMMANDER.
CHALMI, WHAT ARE YOU DOING?
FLYING THIS SHIP HAS BEEN INTERESTING, BUT I CAN'T LET THE PROFESSOR FORCE MY FRIENDS AND FAMILY TO LEAVE HOME. I HAVE TO STOP HIM.
STOP HIM... HOW?
YOU WILL SEE.
THE SHIP IS CHARGING ITS WEAPONS.

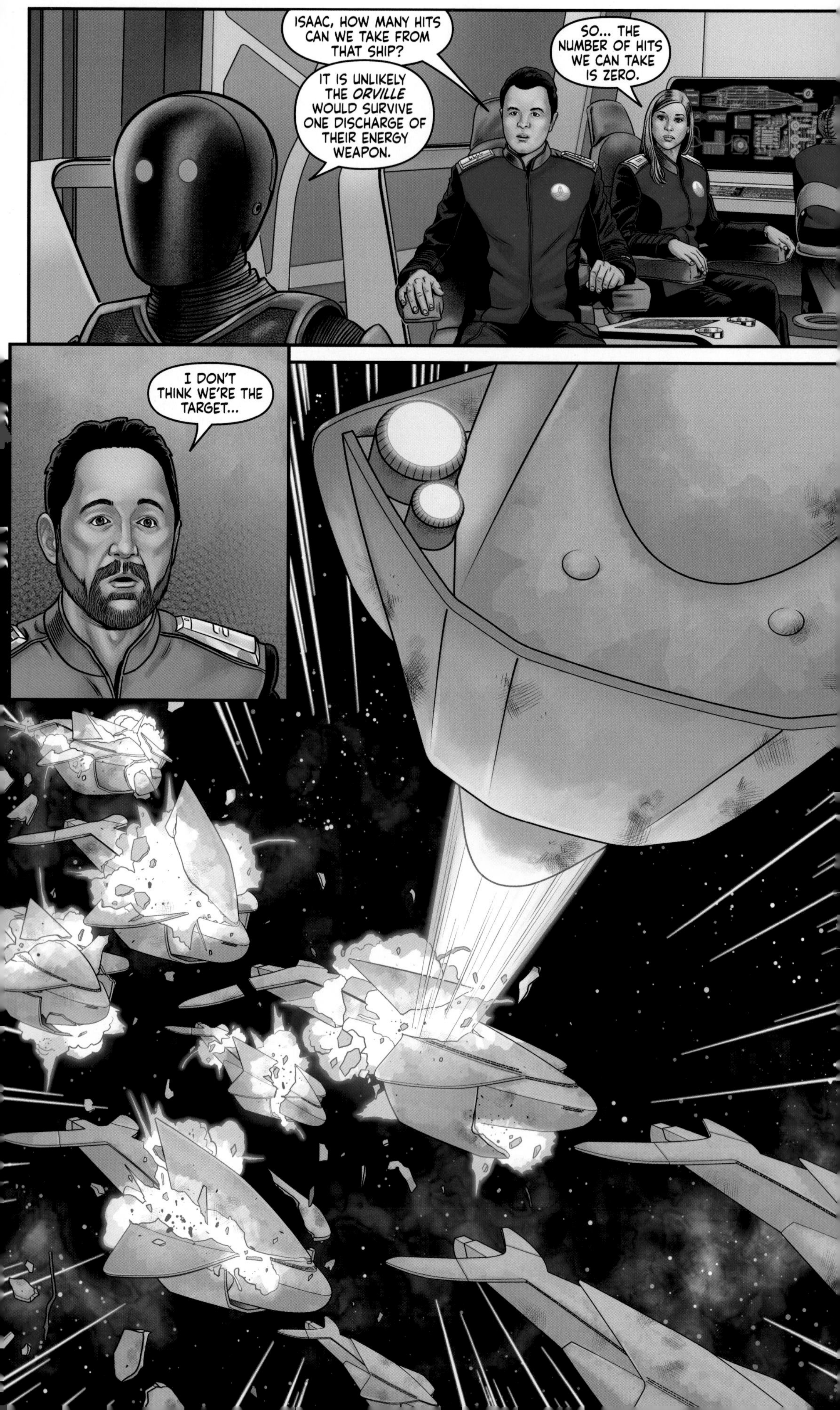
ISAAC, HOW MANY HITS CAN WE TAKE FROM THAT SHIP?
IT IS UNLIKELY THE *ORVILLE* WOULD SURVIVE ONE DISCHARGE OF THEIR ENERGY WEAPON.
SO... THE NUMBER OF HITS WE CAN TAKE IS ZERO.
I DON'T THINK WE'RE THE TARGET...

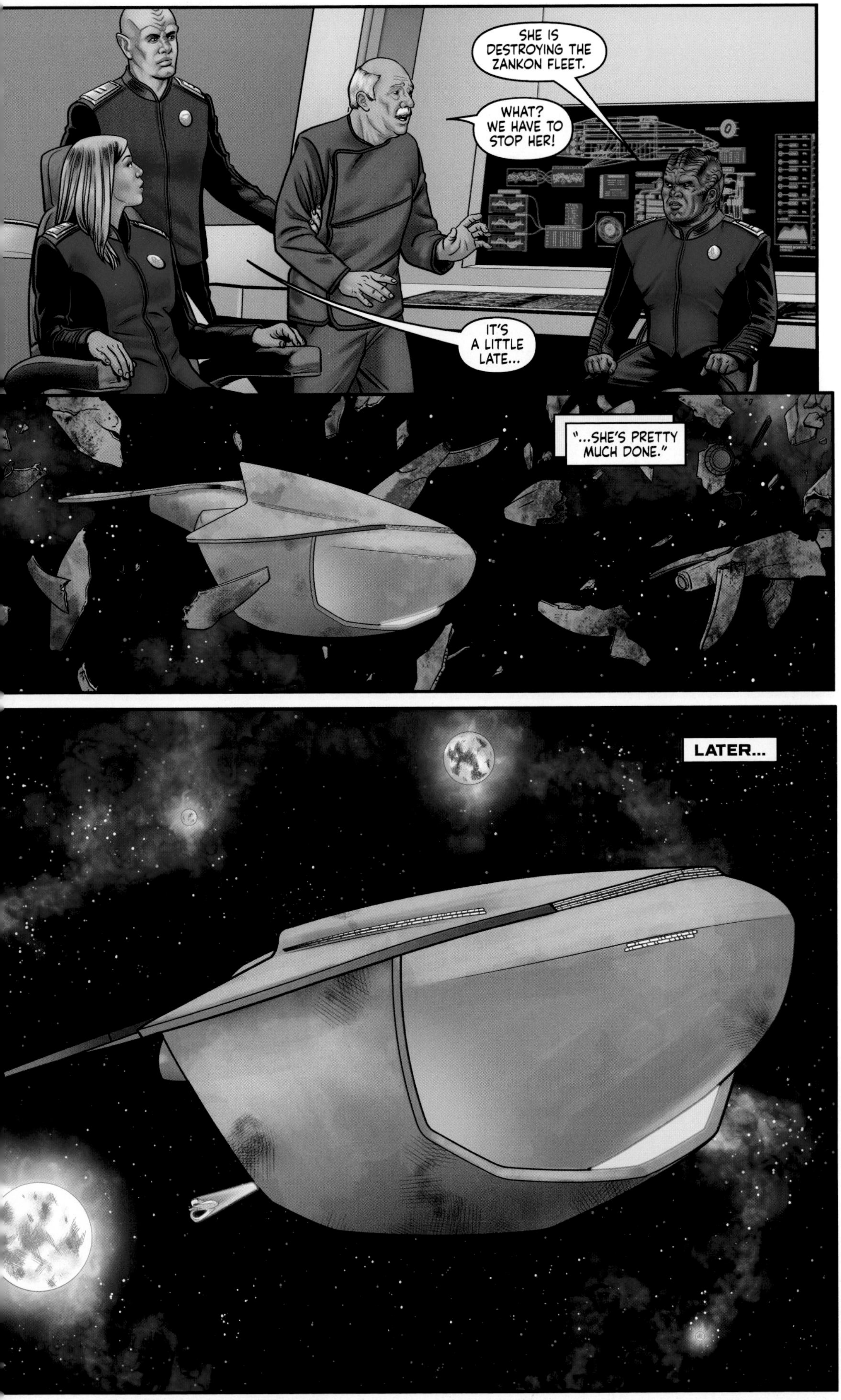
SHE IS DESTROYING THE ZANKON FLEET.
WHAT? WE HAVE TO STOP HER!
IT'S A LITTLE LATE...
"...SHE'S PRETTY MUCH DONE."
LATER...

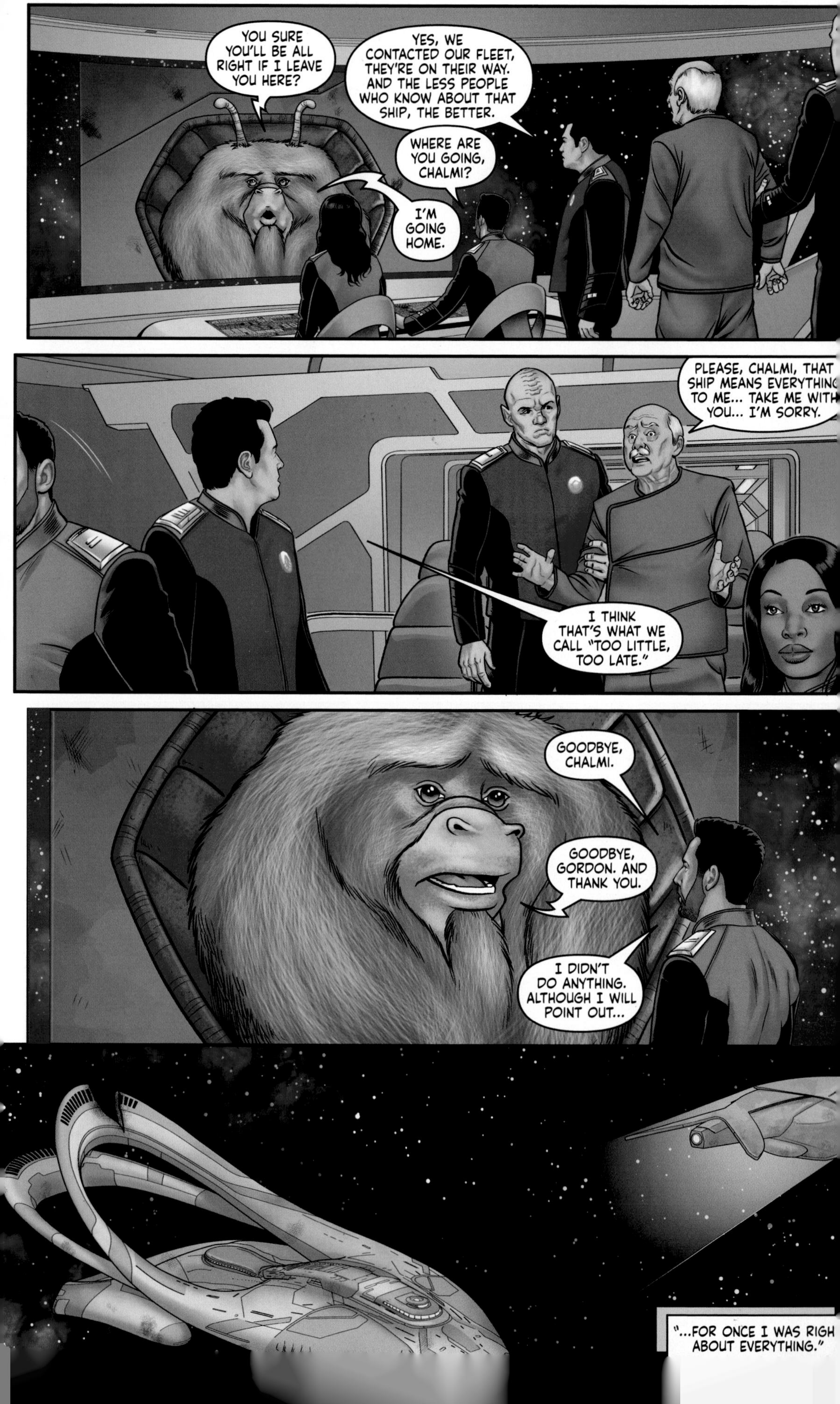
YOU SURE YOU'LL BE ALL RIGHT IF I LEAVE YOU HERE?
YES, WE CONTACTED OUR FLEET, THEY'RE ON THEIR WAY. AND THE LESS PEOPLE WHO KNOW ABOUT THAT SHIP, THE BETTER.
WHERE ARE YOU GOING, CHALMI?
I'M GOING HOME.
PLEASE, CHALMI, THAT SHIP MEANS EVERYTHIN TO ME... TAKE ME WIT YOU... I'M SORRY.
I THINK THAT'S WHAT WE CALL "TOO LITTLE, TOO LATE."
GOODBYE, CHALMI.
GOODBYE, GORDON. AND THANK YOU.
I DIDN'T DO ANYTHING. ALTHOUGH I WILL POINT OUT...
"...FOR ONCE I WAS RIGH ABOUT EVERYTHING."

EARLY SKETCHES BY DAVID CABEZA

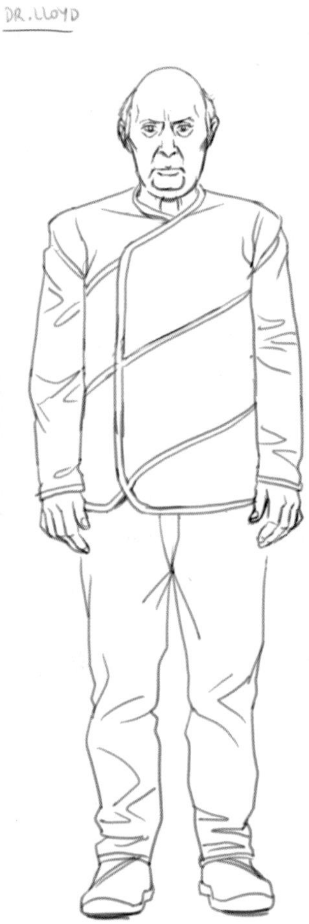
DR. LLOYD

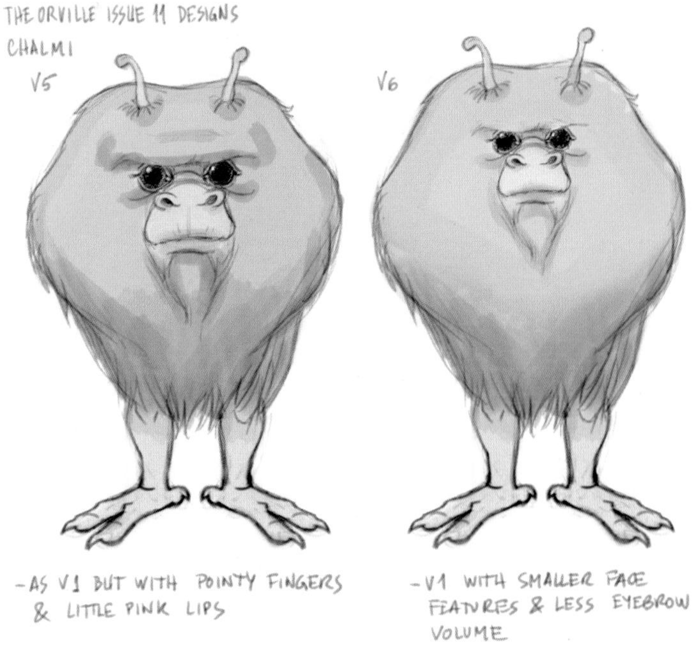
THE ORVILLE ISSUE 11 DESIGNS
CHALMI
V5
V6
- AS V1 BUT WITH POINTY FINGERS & LITTLE PINK LIPS
- V1 WITH SMALLER FACE FEATURES & LESS EYEBROW VOLUME

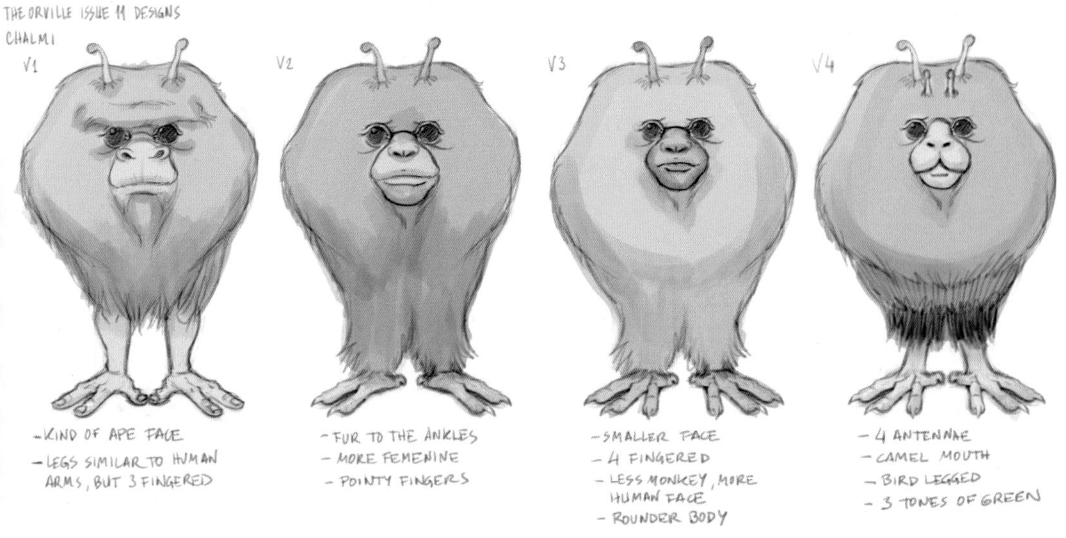
THE ORVILLE ISSUE 11 DESIGNS
CHALMI
V1
V2
V3
V4
- KIND OF APE FACE
- LEGS SIMILAR TO HUMAN ARMS, BUT 3 FINGERED
- FUR TO THE ANKLES
- MORE FEMENINE
- POINTY FINGERS
- SMALLER FACE
- 4 FINGERED
- LESS MONKEY, MORE HUMAN FACE
- ROUNDER BODY
- 4 ANTENNAE
- CAMEL MOUTH
- BIRD LEGGED
- 3 TONES OF GREEN

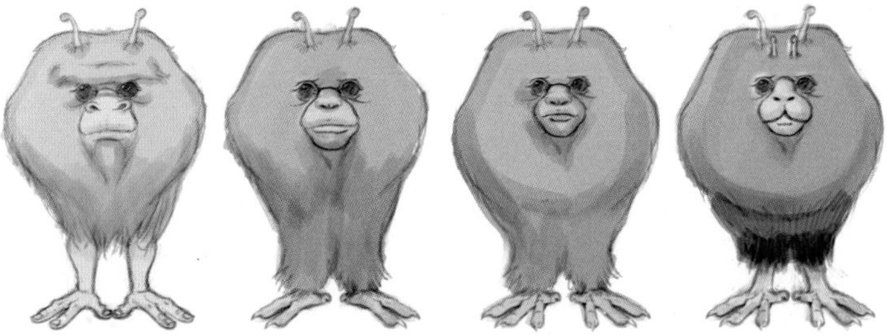

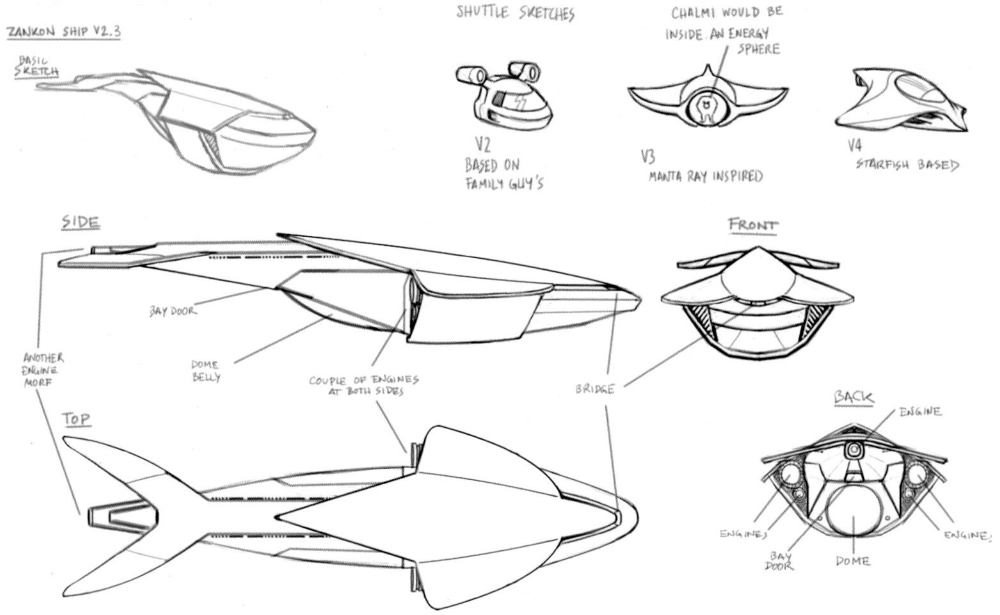
ZANKON SHIP V2.3
BASIC SKETCH
SHUTTLE SKETCHES
CHALMI WOULD BE INSIDE AN ENERGY SPHERE
V2
BASED ON FAMILY GUY'S
V3
MANTA RAY INSPIRED
V4
STARFISH BASED
SIDE
FRONT
BAY DOOR
ANOTHER ENGINE MORF
DOME BELLY
COUPLE OF ENGINES AT BOTH SIDES
BRIDGE
TOP
BACK
ENGINE
ENGINES
BAY DOOR
DOME
ENGINES

THE ORVILLE ISSUE 11 DESIGNS – ZANKON SHIPS

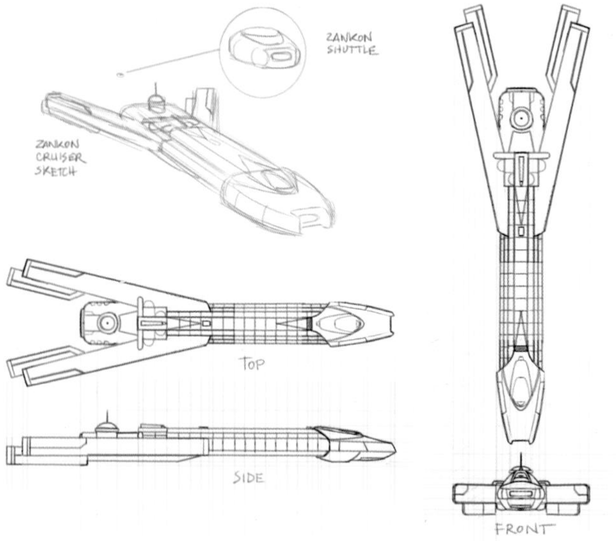
ZANKON SHUTTLE
ZANKON CRUISER SKETCH
TOP
SIDE
FRONT

THE ORVILLE 11
ZANKON SHIP INTERIORS

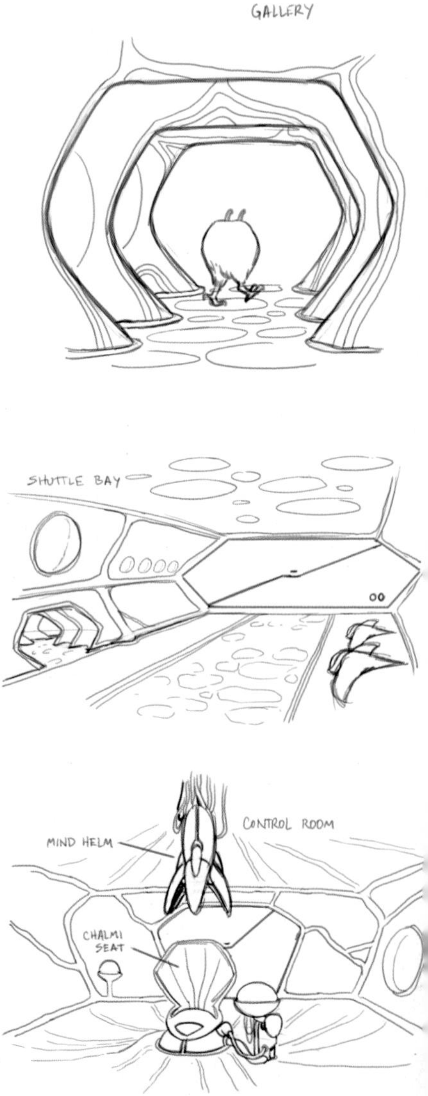
GALLERY
SHUTTLE BAY
MIND HELM
CONTROL ROOM
CHALMI SEAT

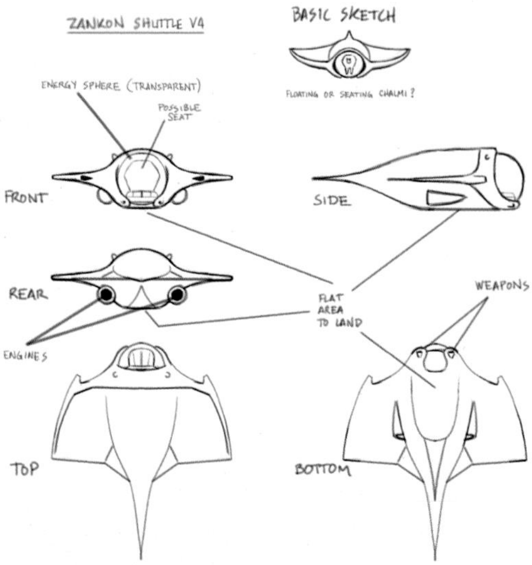
ZANKON SHUTTLE V4
BASIC SKETCH
FLOATING OR SEATING CHALMI?
ENERGY SPHERE (TRANSPARENT)
POSSIBLE SEAT
FRONT
SIDE
REAR
FLAT AREA TO LAND
WEAPONS
ENGINES
TOP
BOTTOM